McPHERSON'S RIDGE

Steven H. Newton

LEO COOPER

Maps on pages 80 and 94 originally appeared in *Stone's Brigade and the Fight for the McPherson Farm*, Combined Publishing/Da Capo Press.
Map on Page 10 originally appeared in *The Gettysburg Campaign*, Combined Publishing/Da Capo Press.

Published under license in Great Britain by

LEO COOPER
an imprint of
Pen & Sword Books Limited
47 Church Street, Barnsley, South Yorkshire S70 2AS

ISBN 0 85052 952 2

A CIP catalogue of this book is available
from the British Library

For up-to-date information on other titles produced under the
Leo Cooper imprint, please telephone or write to:
Pen & Sword Books Ltd, FREEPOST, 47 Church Street,
Barnsley, South Yorkshire S70 2AS
Telephone 01226 734222

McPHERSON'S RIDGE

BATTLEGROUND AMERICA GUIDES offer a unique approach to the battles and battlefields of America. Each book in the series highlights a small American battlefield—sometimes a small portion of a much larger battlefield. All of the units, important individuals, and actions of each engagement on the battlefield are described in a clear and concise narrative. Detailed maps complement the text and illustrate small unit action at each stage of the battle. Historical images and modern-day photographs tie the dramatic events of the past to today's battlefield site and highlight the importance of terrain in battle. The present-day battlefield is described in detail with suggestions for touring the site.

CONTENTS

Introduction   7

Chapter 1   They'll Come Early in the Morning   11

Chapter 2   The Object Being to Feel the Enemy   23

Chapter 3   Tell the General That We Will Hold   33

Chapter 4   Balls Whistled Round Our Heads Like Hail   45

Chapter 5   As Only Brave Men Can Fight   55

Chapter 6   It Was the Intention to Defend the Place   65

Chapter 7   Sprayed by the Brains of the First Rank   77

Chapter 8   A Furious Musketry Fire   87

Chapter 9   Not A Shadow of A Chance   95

Touring the Battlefield   105

Index   115

INTRODUCTION

The map is not the terrain.

Absent real combat experience, the ridges and ravines of Fort A. P. Hill, just south of the Rappahannock River, taught me that lesson over and over again as a platoon sergeant attempting to maneuver vehicles and troops through simulated battles. Further south, near Blackstone, Virginia, Fort Pickett reinforced the learning curve. In the 1990s we used topographical maps that still showed a World War II-era hospital complex below the main cantonment area, even though the buildings were long gone, the concrete slabs almost entirely covered with tangled undergrowth, and the neatly patterned streets had long since been submerged somewhere beneath tree roots. It was a great place to send brand-new lieutenants with a compass and a map.

At the beginning of the twenty-first century American soldiers employ compasses, computer-generated topographic maps, and global positioning satellites to assist our troops in figuring out where they are, what's over the next ridge, where the enemy might be hiding, and the proper coordinates to call for artillery fire. Even so, with all the high-tech marvels, each generation of fighters has to relearn that essential lesson: the map is not the terrain.

I can still remember one young squad leader, standing adamantly with her feet spread apart and her hands on her hips in the middle of a five-road intersection. The map told her that the intersection had four roads (and a building on one corner), and was located about two hundred meters *over there.* Her GPS system (after it finally located sufficient satellites to express an opinion) archly informed her that she was really standing forty meters north of the intersection, on the ridgeline I could see over her shoulder. Her squad (many of whom had more years time in the service than she did) had taken an impromptu break while she considered the evidence. Eventually, she looked at me, and said, "Damn it, Sergeant, according to the map and the GPS, this intersection isn't here!" I asked her which one she thought was more likely to be correct, the map, the satellite, or the pavement beneath her feet.

Civil War soldiers, from privates to commanding generals, had to learn about maps and terrain the hard way: quickly, while other people died. Major General George McClellan predicated his entire plan to advance up the James-York peninsula from Fortress Monroe to Richmond on the information he saw on a map that depicted the main road running parallel to the Warwick River rather than across it. At Chancellorsville, Lieutenant General Thomas J. "Stonewall" Jackson launched the attack that defeated the Army of the Potomac by leading his entire corps through the Wilderness on a road that did not appear on Federal maps. But most flank marches ended quite differently, as guides somehow failed to know their home counties and officers led their men down the wrong trails.

Part of the confusion stemmed from map-making conventions of the period. Instead of the neat contour lines delineating the slope and shape of hillsides, nineteenth-century cartographers more often used what could be called the "fuzzy caterpillar" approach to drawing mountains, hills, and ridges. When well executed, such maps could give an excellent overall "feel" for the terrain, and are in fact often easier to use for three-dimensional visualization than modern topographic conventions. But those maps never satisfactorily answered questions like "Where's the highest point on this ridge?" or "Exactly which of these furry little brush strokes does the colonel want me to occupy, and how do I find it?"

At Gettysburg, for all three days of America's most celebrated battle, the terrain played an exceptionally critical role in determining the course of the fighting and the ultimate outcome of the battle. General Robert E. Lee, Major General George G. Meade, and their senior officers based their plans on what maps, reports from staff officers, and the view through their own field glasses could tell them. Those plans were conveyed to the colonels commanding regiments and the captains leading companies, most of whom would fight the entire battle without ever seeing a map of the relevant Pennsylvania countryside. They nonetheless had to take their commanders' often second- or third-hand understanding of the terrain and work it out on the ground while other people were shooting at them. The resulting struggles for the Round Tops, Cemetery Hill, Culp's Hill, and Cemetery Ridge decided the battle.

Yet there might not have been a battle at all, at least not at Gettysburg, if not for McPherson's Ridge.

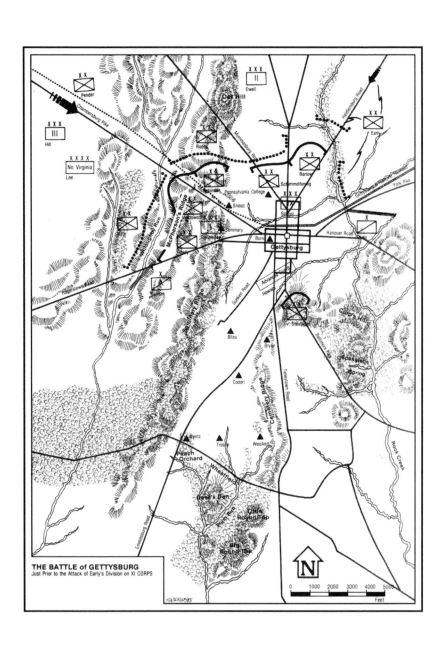

THE BATTLE of GETTYSBURG
Just Prior to the Attack of Early's Division on XI CORPS

CHAPTER 1

THEY'LL COME EARLY IN THE MORNING

FAR FEWER THAN HALF OF THE VISITORS to Gettysburg who take the self-guided tour elect to take the short drive north-west of town to visit McPherson's Ridge. Those who do make the right turn off Route 116—the old Hagerstown Pike—and spend a few minutes on what is known today as Reynolds Avenue. In the summer heat many do not even get out of their cars, while others stop and photograph a few monuments (often with their children standing on the bases) before driving around the circle made by Buford and Doubleday Avenues that takes them past Oak Hill and the Eternal Light Peace Memorial. A few intrepid souls dis-mount their vehicles long enough to scamper down and examine the railroad cut, but it is possible to pass an entire afternoon without seeing more than one or two figures actually looking out across McPherson's Ridge as the cav-alry and artillerymen would have done on the morning of July 1, 1863; nor does anyone usually glance over his or her shoulder and realize just how close the Gettysburg Seminary and the town itself stands to their position. Instead, most visitors make short work of McPherson's Ridge and the first day's fight before navigating back across their folded maps to more famous places: Devil's Den, Little Round Top, Cemetery Ridge. . . .

The problem is not one of callousness or apathy, but ter-rain. Driving down Reynolds Avenue, McPherson's could be any one of thousands of gently rolling ridges that cut across the farms and fields of central Pennsylvania, and

Willoughby Run appears to be an inconsequential trickle. Appreciating the significance of McPherson's Ridge and the action fought for its possession that steamy July day requires a soldier's view of the land around Gettysburg. And the soldier's view is not that of the commanding generals. A single glance at the map revealed Gettysburg as a critical strategic point for defeating the Confederate invasion of Pennsylvania. Before his relief as commander of the Army of the Potomac, Major General Joseph Hooker had based his operational plan in part on controlling the junction of the ten major roads passing through the town. His successor, Major General George G. Meade—a Pennsylvanian—knew the area as well, sending forward orders to his cavalry in late June "to hold Gettysburg at all hazards until supports arrive." A possibly apocryphal anecdote even has Mary Todd Lincoln, flitting through the Washington D. C. telegraph office, stopping dead in her tracks as she looked at the map, and picking out Gettysburg as "a spider spinning its web." The army that controlled Gettysburg could maneuver in any direction; of course, it could also be attacked from any direction as well.

A corps or division commander, however, went where he was sent and made the best out of the ground assigned to him. Aided by his scouts and engineers, these officers had to move from the abstract two-dimensional representation provided (often quite inaccurately) by his maps to a three-dimensional understanding of the actual terrain—"The map is not the terrain." However stated, this premise has been an integral component of the education of military officers since Hannibal braved the Alps, George Washington's boats picked through the ice on the Delaware River, or Captain Robert E. Lee found his way through the brush to find an unknown track around the Mexican position at Cerro Gordo. Someone with a trained eye (and good binoculars, if possible) has to stand on the crest of the hills to see what can be seen. If the line is posted *there*, do dead angles exist in which the enemy can creep close without our being able to bring him under fire? Should the battery be deployed on *that* crest? From which hills can even heavier rifled guns make firing or even survival possible? Where are the flanks? Where is the line of retreat? How many men should be held in reserve?

When Brigadier General John Buford, the thirty-seven-year-old Kentuckian (West Point, 1848) who commanded the Army of the Potomac's 1st Cavalry Division, rode into Gettysburg around noon on June 30, 1863, he already knew that everyone above him in the chain of command considered possession of the town vital to Union interests. Lee's Army of Northern Virginia had stolen a march on the Federals while Hooker, General-in-Chief Henry Halleck, and President Abraham Lincoln had been quarreling over the prerogatives of command. By the time Meade received the order that made him Hooker's successor (about 3:00 A.M. on June 28), Lee's army had spread itself in a wide arc across central Pennsylvania from Chambersburg to York, while the Army of the Potomac remained at least a dozen miles south of the Maryland border. Whoever held Gettysburg—and to a lesser extent, Hanover—would be able to dictate much of the future course of the campaign to his opponent, but Meade admitted to Major General John F. Reynolds of the I Corps on July 1 that the terrain there was still a mystery to him. He was "not sufficiently well informed of the nature of the country to judge of its character for either an offensive or defensive position."

Reynolds had just been assigned command of the army's left wing, thirty-two thousand troops of the I, III, and XI Corps, who represented the troops closest to Gettysburg. A Pennsylvanian, the forty-two-year-old Reynolds embodied personal bravery, tactical acumen, outstanding horsemanship, and the ability to curse imaginatively enough to hold everyone's attention. Ironically, Reynolds could have been commanding the Army of the Potomac that summer instead of Meade; Lincoln had recently offered him the post. Having witnessed the political infighting that went with army command, however, Reynolds had insisted on a guarantee that his civil and military superiors in Washington would not interfere with his operations, something that Lincoln would not and could not give. Reynolds thus declined the offer, and loyally supported Meade's appointment. Having grown up in Lancaster, just fifty miles from Gettysburg, Reynolds understood the importance of the town's position in the regional road network, but not having reached Gettysburg himself, Reynolds had to rely on Buford's assessment of the local terrain.

John Buford was a hard-fighting, plain-spoken cavalryman, whose "uniform" usually consisted of an ancient hunting shirt "ornamented with holes," plain corduroy pants, and cowboy boots. A contemporary pictured Buford as "a compactly built man of middle height with a tawny mustache and little, triangular grey eye, whose expression is determined, not to say sinister. . . . He is of a good natured disposition, but not to be trifled with." A trooper in the 8th Illinois Cavalry commented "He don't put on so much style as most officers," but the general was "always on hand when there is fighting to be done. . . ." His scrawled notes in the midst of any operation provided blunt, unadorned impressions of the tactical situation as he saw it. Once, during the Gettysburg campaign, he sent his corps chief of staff a message that, lacking any formal salutation, began with "I have had a very rough day of it."

At Gettysburg on June 30, Buford "found everybody in a terrible state of excitement on account of the enemy's advance," but reported that Rebel strength was "terribly exaggerated by reasonable and truthful but inexperienced men." After chasing off some Confederate foragers, he advised his superiors that "I can't do much just now. My men and horses are fagged out," and his wagons had been left behind at Mechanicsville. He had no grain: "It is all in the country and the people talk instead of working." But by that night, Buford had learned that the Confederates were both nearer and stronger than he had originally thought. At

General John Buford.

(Harper's Weekly)

least two divisions of Lieutenant General A. P. Hill's III Corps of the Army of Northern Virginia—estimated at nine thousand men each—were "massed back of Cashtown, nine miles from this place," while another division from Lieutenant General Richard Ewell's II Corps had been reported moving south from Carlisle. "Should I have to fall back, advise me by what route," Buford asked Reynolds. Falling back represented a very real possibility, given that between them his two brigades mounted only 2,750 exhausted troopers, supported by six three-inch guns.

Buford sent this message at 10:40 P.M., knowing that no reply would be forthcoming before morning, and equally aware that the aggressive Reynolds was just as likely to order the town held as evacuated. Buford, after all, could read those strategic maps as well as his superiors. So he conducted his own tactical reconnaisance, becoming the

Buford's cavalry holding the Union line at Willoughby Run in some of the opening action at Gettysburg.

first senior officer in the Army of the Potomac to assess the terrain at Gettysburg. The best defensive line obviously lay south of town, in the peculiar "fishhook" configuration running from Culp's Hill down Cemetery Ridge to the Round Tops. "Lovely ground" is what novelist Michael Shaara imagined Buford thought when he saw it. Those hills and ridges could be turned into an impregnable bastion by Federal infantry, but the line was far too long for two cavalry brigades (even armed with repeating carbines), with nothing else like it for miles to the south. If he made his stand there and lost the hills before the infantry arrived, Reynolds and Meade would have forfeited Gettysburg before a battle even truly got started.

Instead, Buford decided to meet the Rebels north and northwest of the town, as far forward from that defensible line as he could get, along a series of rolling ridges where cavalry might win more time in a delaying action than a stand-up fight. This was not an easy decision, for it courted the outright destruction of his entire division if he miscalculated. He had courted a similar fate at Second Manassas, in a running fight over several ridges at Lewis Farm, which had ended with his brigade in a panicked flight, himself badly wounded and left for dead; Buford knew he could not allow his division to be stampeded the next day, not here. One signal officer, Lieutenant Aaron Jerome, thought his commander "seemed anxious, even more so than I ever saw him."

Buford ordered Colonel Thomas C. Devin to cover the northern approaches to Gettysburg with his 2nd Cavalry Brigade, picketing from Mummasburg Road west across Herr Ridge Road toward the Carlisle and Harrisburg Pikes. The 1,150 men of the 6th and 9th New York, 17th Pennsylvania, and two companies of the 3rd West Virginia assumed responsibility for dealing with the arrival of any units of Ewell's II Corps, an assignment that would bring them their own share of hard fighting, but which also took them out of most of the upcoming struggle for McPherson's Ridge. This arrangement also staked everything on timely reinforcement by Reynolds's infantry: with both brigades thrown forward, Buford's headquarters guard effectively constituted the entire division reserve.

Colonel William Gamble, a forty-five-year-old Irishman, commanded Buford's 1st Brigade, which consisted of sixteen hundred men from the 8th Illinois, four companies of the 12th Illinois, six companies of the 3rd Indiana, and the 8th New York. By trade a civil engineer in Chicago, during his early life Gamble had been employed in the Queen's Surveying Office of the Royal Engineers, done a short hitch as a dragoon in the British Army, and—upon immigrating to America—spent five years in the 1st U. S. Dragoons. Before his enlistment expired, the young soldier had fought Seminoles in Florida and explored the west with John C.

17

Fremont. Gamble had been severely wounded at Malvern Hill the previous year when commanding the 8th Illinois Cavalry, and took over the brigade from the talented Colonel Benjamin "Grimes" Davis, who had been killed at Brandy Station only in June. He thus represented an essentially unknown quantity at this level. On the other hand, Gamble had impressed his division commander with both his confidence and aggressiveness in personally leading a charge a week earlier at Upperville; "I'll be damned if I can't whip a little corner of hell with that First Brigade," Buford had said.

Buford's deployment of Gamble's brigade clearly illustrated his plan for delaying any Confederate advance and his assessment of the terrain northwest of Gettysburg. Closest to the town itself, he placed his division's main camps along Seminary Ridge, intended to be a final fall-back position if it became necessary to retreat through the

Present-day photo of the Federal artillery position on McPherson's Ridge. The northern edge of Gettysburg is in the background.

streets and south toward Cemetery Hill. About four hundred yards west of his camps ran McPherson's Ridge, atop which Buford placed the six three-inch guns of Battery A, 2nd U. S. Artillery, commanded by Lieutenant John H. Calef. Calef had two guns north of the Chambersburg Pike, two immediately south of that road, and the final two down the ridge toward the Hagerstown Pike. The ground west of the artillery position sloped down into Willoughby Run, which meandered along the marshy bottom separating McPherson's Ridge from Herr Ridge. Calef's gunners therefore had predominantly rolling fields in front of them, with one significant exception. Roughly three hundred yards south of the Chambersburg Pike stood McPherson's Woods (also known as the Herbst Woods), several dozen acres of forest beginning just west of McPherson's Ridge and extending down to the creek. Another thirteen hundred yards west of McPherson's, on partially wooded Herr Ridge, was where Buford intended to locate Gamble's main skirmish line, with the bulk of his brigade between the Fairfield Road and the Hagerstown Pike. Colonel George Chapman led the two squadrons of the 12th Illinois and 3rd Indiana at the northern end of the line; Major John Beveridge held the center with Gamble's own 8th Illinois; and Lieutenant Colonel William Markell's 8th New York took the left flank. Given the necessity of using every fourth man as a horse-holder and throwing out videttes even further, the 1st Brigade would have to man a mile-long front with only about five to seven hundred dismounted cavalry.

Over two hundred videttes, who constituted Buford's earliest warning of a Rebel advance, had been dispatched nearly four miles out from Gettysburg along every main axis of advance on a front nearly four and one-half miles wide, with patrols riding regularly between the individual posts. This represented an exceptionally farflung and attenuated line, but Buford was conscious of many conflicting reports of the location of Hill's III Corps, so "I have to pay attention to some of them, which causes me to over work my horses and men." Buford intended to discover the Confederate approach early, giving him time to deploy Gamble's regiments to Herr Ridge, where—despite their relatively small numbers—their concentrated fire would force even a Rebel infantry division to take time to change from column into line of battle, push forward skirmishers, and force them off the heights. Under cover of Calef's guns, the Yankee cavalry could then retire across Willoughby Run to McPherson's Ridge faster than Hill's footsoldiers could follow, allowing him to set up a new defensive line and start the process anew.

Buford knew quite clearly that he could not hold either ridge against a determined Confederate attack, though Devin thought otherwise. At a conference late in the evening of June 30, the brigadier told his commander, "You're unduly excited, General. I'll agree to take care of all the rebels that come from the directions you indicate for the next 24 hours." When Buford answered, he must have been remembering a year earlier, when his own brigade had been left holding Thoroughfare Gap, waiting for infantry that never arrived. He told his overconfident subordinate, "No you won't. They'll come early in the morning, with skirmishers three deep, and you'll have to fight like the devil to hold your own till support arrives. . . ." What little if any fitful sleep John Buford got that night had to be haunted by the thought of juggling time and distance in the face of dauntingly superior numbers; having made his "arrangements . . . for entertaining him until General Reynolds could reach the scene," all the Kentuckian could do now was wait.

The videttes, miles distant, also waited. The night was probably foggy, with vaguely luminous though threateningly opaque white shapes lingering in the bottomlands. Some of the men could no doubt spot distant Rebel campfires, but closer in—even where there was no mist—hearing rather than sight became the critical sense. Night vision, as modern soldiers think of it, was generally absent among Civil War soldiers, because poor rations and physical exhaustion insidiously sapped their eyes' ability to adjust to low light conditions. The tired blue-clad cavalrymen, huddled in little knots of two or three comrades with one awake and the others stealing catnaps, would have heard ominous sounds throughout the hours of darkness. Did the clank of metal and the muffled sound of hoofbeats mean that their own patrols were making another circuit, or had enemy horsemen ventured out in the night? Often the distance or direction of such noises was impossible to determine, leaving the troops in a constant edgy, increasingly fatigued state.

Added to these physical realities were the fears and uncertainties faced by many of the Army of the Potomac's soldiers that night. Another army commander had been relieved; Meade to them was an unknown entity, and there were even rumors that McClellan was being recalled yet again. After disaster at Chancellorsville and a moment of sweet revenge for the Federal cavalry at Brandy Station, the war had abruptly been transferred into Union territory. Lee had stolen a march on their generals again, leaving the cavalry sitting in the dark, miles ahead of the infantry, waiting for the next desperate fight. They trusted Buford—he was a cavalryman to the core—and most had begun to develop good impressions of Gamble as well. Survival tomorrow, however, not to mention the difference between victory and shattering defeat, really lay in the hands of officers and troops they did not know half so well: John Reynolds, Abner Doubleday, James Wadsworth, and the divisions of the I Corps. Buford thought of trading distance for time; the men in the dark knew he would have to trade some of their lives as well.

At 7:30 A.M. the waiting ended. Lieutenant Marcellus Jones of Company E, 8th Illinois Cavalry, rode up to a vidette post on Knoxlyn Ridge above Marsh Creek on the Hagerstown Pike to investigate a report that the Rebels were coming. Private Thomas Kelley led Jones to a point overlooking the bridge, and gestured toward a Confederate line in column some seven hundred yards distant, led by an officer on a grey horse. Picking up his carbine, Private George Sager prepared to try for a long, lucky shot, but Jones stopped him. "Hold on, George," the young lieutenant said, "give me the honor of opening this ball." With a grim smile, Jones borrowed a weapon and fired the first (missed) shot at Gettysburg.

The word filtered back quickly; horse-holder Leander Warren later recalled that in Gamble's camps "the bugles began to blow and the men got their horses ready. . . ." At that moment Lieutenant Colonel John Kress, a staff officer from the 1st Division, I Corps, rode up to Buford's headquarters. As he sent his own officers into action, Buford asked Kress pointedly, "What are you doing here, sir?" When Kress explained that he had been sent ahead to locate some shoes for his division, Buford told him abruptly that he had better get back to his outfit immediately.

"Why, what's the matter, General?"

Before Buford could answer, the sound of a single cannon sounded to the west. Mounting his horse, the cavalryman looked down at the confused staffer and said with a grim smile, "*That's* the matter."

CHAPTER 2

The Object Being to Feel the Enemy

YEARS AFTER THE FACT, when they had become accustomed to thinking of those three days at Gettysburg as being the Confederacy's "High Tide," veterans of the Army of Northern Virginia frequently described the Pennsylvanian countryside through which they tramped that summer with nostalgic fondness. William F. Fulton II of the 5th Alabama Battalion remembered that he and his comrades "were struck with the similarity of the farms and farm houses, all made after the same pattern." The sturdy red barns—"sometimes better than the dwellings of the owners"—also impressed the soldiers from the Deep South, and "the clover and wheat fields looked very enticing to us who were from the cotton fields of Alabama." Though he emphasized to his descendants that Lee had given strict orders that "there was to be no meddling with that which belonged to private citizens, under penalty of severe punishment," Fulton almost sheepishly admitted that "soldiers seemed to consider chickens and fruits of all kinds to be exempt from this general order." Historians would more dispassionately add country hams, fence rails, hats, shoes, horses, and even free black citizens to the list.

The four companies of Major Arthur van de Graaf's 5th Alabama Battalion belonged to Brigadier General James J. Archer's Brigade, Heth's Division, Hill's III Corps; their fourteen officers and one hundred and twenty-one soldiers (along with two companies of the 13th Alabama) unwittingly became the Confederate vanguard marching toward Gettysburg on July 1. Experienced, confident, and fresh from an astounding though costly victory at Chancellorsville, van de Graaf's troops and the other 7,326 officers and men of Heth's Division exemplified many of the problems underlying the recent reorganization of the Army of Northern Virginia. Following the death of Lieutenant General Thomas J. "Stonewall" Jackson at Chancellorsville, Lee had divided the army into three corps of three divisions each. To create the new III Corps (which he tapped A. P. Hill to command), the Virginian had transferred Major General Richard Anderson's Division from the I Corps, broken up Hill's old Light Division, and added two new brigades of North Carolinians and Mississippians. The four best brigades of the Light Division had been kept together under Major General William Dorsey Pender, while the remaining two had been consolidated with the newcomers to form a division for Henry Heth.

A thirty-eight-year-old Virginian with the right family connections, Heth was also a professional soldier, having

General Henry Heth.
(Library of Congress)

24

graduated from West Point in 1837—albeit last in a class of thirty-eight cadets. Minor assignments in the Appalachian mountains had been followed by a fortuitous transfer to the Army of Northern Virginia just prior to Chancellors-ville, where seniority vaulted him over several more experienced officers to temporary division command when casualties decimated the II Corps's senior leadership. Heth performed well enough in the emergency that he was rewarded with the army's newest division. Unfortunately, a few days in confused combat had not revealed the salient truth about Heth's generalship. Though possessing the right education and the proper pedigree, Henry Heth never fulfilled his early promise. He remained, throughout his career, an overly optimistic battlefield tactician, prone to ignore prudence and consistently willing to make uncoordinated attacks without consulting his superiors. (On a more positive personal note, neither during nor after the war did Heth make any pretensions to military genius, and freely admitted most—if not all—of his tactical gaffes as a division commander.) That July morning he would act for far too long on the mistaken supposition that the only Yankees around Gettysburg were elderly militia with anti-quated muskets. Having told Hill that he intended to send his brigades into town to find some shoes for his barefoot troops, Heth lacked the mental flexibility to adapt to a new and dangerous situation.

Had Heth been supported by a veteran division with experienced brigadiers his own shortcomings would not have figured so decisively in the engagement to come. Johnston J. Pettigrew, the senior brigade commander, had plenty of tactical skills, but he and his North Carolinians were too new to the army to have developed a strong working relationship with their comrades. The other recent arrival, Joseph Davis, brought three solid regiments of Mississippi troops and another outfit of Tarheels to Lee's army; Davis himself, however, owed his position not to experience or talent but to the fact that the president of the Confederacy was his uncle. Not having participated in the army's recent battles, these two brigades composed two-thirds of the division's strength. And the veteran brigades, still smarting at their transfer out of the Light Division, had their own shortcomings. Four small (just 971 strong), unhappy Virginia units marched into battle under the temporary command of Colonel John Brockenbrough, a dour, humorless man who had little feeling for maintaining his brigade's morale and even less for battlefield maneuvers.

Finally, there was Archer's Alabama–Tennessee brigade, 1,197 veterans who had been thoroughly bloodied in every fight from the Peninsula forward, and who had seen few replacements sent out to make good their losses. The 5th Alabama Battalion, 13th Alabama, and 1st, 7th, and 14th Tennessee had done themselves proud at Chancellorsville, capturing a key position at Hazel Grove on May 3, but the engagement, Archer noted, cost "in killed & wounded more than a fourth of my brigade. . . ." Overlooked after the battle was the fact that Archer had lost control of his regiments in tangled terrain, to be saved primarily by the quick thinking of the 1st Tennessee's Colonel Newton George. A handsome forty-five-year-old Marylander (nicknamed "Sally" for his good looks during his college days), Archer had been a volunteer in the Mexican War before quitting his law practice to join the Regular army in 1855 without the benefit of a West Point education. He had been mustered into Confederate service as colonel of the 5th Texas, a varied enough background to make him an acceptable leader for a brigade composed of men from different states. Two factors would affect Archer's performance the morning of July 1, 1863: a fever that left him somewhat weakened and the lack of a strong rapport with his new division commander. In fifty years, no one has improved on the observation about Heth's Division made by historian Clifford Dowdey: "The two weakest brigades numerically, one under dubious leadership, were joined to the new brigades to form a division under the second-best division commander, who was himself still unproved."

Archer roused his men at 5:00 A.M., and with the Alabama troops leading the brigade came down the Chambersburg Pike around 7:30. Private E. T. Boland of the 13th Alabama recalled over thirty years later that as his regiment was about to cross the Marsh Creek Bridge he saw several Yankee cavalrymen a few hundred yards off to his right. That this was Lieutenant Jones and the outpost of the 8th Illinois was proven moments later when a single round whizzed past the Rebel line. News of this chance encounter passed back through the Confederate ranks. Colonel Birkett D. Fry of the 13th Alabama, reported Captain J. B. Tunney, "rode back to the color bearer and ordered him to uncase the colors, the first intimation that we had that we were about to engage the enemy." Heth, apparently riding with the brigade, directed Archer to throw out skirmishers south of Chambersburg Pike, but—still convinced that the mounted men across Marsh Creek were home guards—instructed the brigade commander to leave the remainder in column so that the march would not be interrupted long. The division commander sent similar orders to Davis, requiring him to deploy skirmishers north of the road.

Van de Graaf's battalion, supported by Companies B and G of the 13th Alabama under Lieutenant Will Crawford fanned out ahead of Archer's Brigade, not quite two hundred men in all. Facing the Alabama troops initially was Company E, 8th Illinois Cavalry—just forty men spread across several hundred yards. The Federals' Spencer repeaters, however, created the impression of a significantly larger force as the Confederates began to push their way through the wheatfields alongside the road. "The true character and length of our line soon became known to the enemy," reported Lieutenant Amasa Dana of the 8th Illinois, "and they promptly moved upon our front and flanks." The Yankees noted with ironic pride, however, that their delaying action caused Heth to order the

Fredericksburg (Virginia) Artillery unlimbered, "and the woods to our rear was shelled vigorously, no one being in range of their shells." Nonetheless, the heavily outnumbered Yankees fell back past several fence lines, as several squadrons of reinforcements arrived to bolster their line and purchase Gamble the necessary minutes to form up the bulk of his brigade on Herr Ridge.

(As the years passed and the veterans' reminiscences grew colored with age, small details emerged that, while they may or may not have been apocryphal, initiated the seemingly inexhaustible pool of human-interest stories surrounding Gettysburg. The first Confederate casualty, for example, was supposedly the canine mascot of Company A, 5th Alabama Battalion rather than any of the soldiers. As if to even matters out, members of the 13th Alabama recorded that a farmer's dog began barking at them, and when he would not quit, "he was shot by several [men], and of course that layed him out." The dog had belonged to a farmer who, seemingly unaware that the war was about to occur across his fields, asked the Rebel skirmishers what was happening. Informed that a battle between "General Lee and the Yankees" was brewing the astonished farmer responded, "Tell Lee to hold on just a little until I get my cow out of the pasture." More prosaically, one of the first Confederate casualties was Private C. L. F. Worley of Company A, 5th Alabama Battalion. Struck in the thigh, Worley would lose his leg on the operating table at a nearby field hospital.)

Gamble had meanwhile concentrated nine hundred men atop Herr Ridge, who fired into Archer's skirmish line as their own videttes retreated. This force actually outnumbered Archer's leading element, but had to be dispersed north of the road as well, to face the two hundred and fifty Mississippi skirmishers fronting Davis's Brigade. The Federal brigade commander realized that he could not possibly make a prolonged stand, since he could already see the main bodies of the two brigades—over forty-four hundred more men—approaching slowly up Chambersburg Pike. As he lowered his field glasses, Gamble realized that, at best, he might convince Heth to waste the time to deploy the remaining regiments of those brigades into line of battle before attacking the ridge. (By the next spring, as often happened with hindsight, Gamble convinced himself that he, not Buford had "select[ed] the most eligible line of battle," and that "we had to fight the whole Army Corps. of Genl. A. P. Hill 25,000 strong for three & ½ hours. . . ." He would complain that "Nothing of this is mentioned in the newspapers or dispatches, but the above are absolute facts under my own observation.")

Unfortunately for Gamble, the Alabama and Mississippi skirmishers knew their jobs, and with artillery support even the rapid-firing Federal carbines could not hold them back. Moving forward in staggered knots of three to five men, the Southerners fired, gauged the enemy response, and then extended their lines to lap the Yankee flanks. With the mass of two brigades in reserve, they could afford to thin the center of their line to an extent the Union horse soldiers could not match. Returning fire from above, even the veteran cavalrymen had a tendency to shoot too high (the 5th Alabama Battalion lost only seven men wounded). About an hour had passed from the initial contact when Gamble reluctantly gave the order to quit Herr Ridge, withdrawing toward Buford's main position along McPherson's Ridge. He left a thin screen of his own skirmishers in the tangled foliage on the banks of Willoughby Run.

Gamble's brief stand on Herr Ridge had not forced Heth to reinforce his skirmish line beyond committing a single battery, but once the Confederate division commander rode to a point from which he could see McPherson's Ridge, his attitude changed. Abruptly Heth realized that a full brigade of Yankee cavalry was now concentrated there—Gamble had twelve hundred men on the ridge with Calef's six guns in support. The Virginian ordered Archer and Davis to deploy their entire brigades, and sent couriers back to alert Pettigrew and Brockenbrough that their troops should be prepared to support the attack. He now believed that somewhere behind Buford's mounted troopers there might be a brigade or two of Union infantry, but with seventy-five hundred men in hand and Pender's Division nearby, Heth told Davis and Archer "to advance, the object being to feel the enemy; to make a forced reconnaissance, and determine in what force the enemy were—whether or not he was massing his forces on Gettysburg." Archer—who had seen considerably more battlefields than his division commander—demurred, considering his brigade too "light to risk so far in advance of support." With some asperity, Heth repeated the order, and a few minutes later (about 9:30 A.M.) Archer's men stepped off, the 13th Alabama on the right flank and the 1st Tennessee, 5th Alabama Battalion, 14th Tennessee, and 7th Tennessee extending the line in that order. The Marylander intended to push rapidly across Willoughby Run to seize McPherson's Woods before the Federals could react. Just north of the Chambersburg Pike, Davis also advanced with seventeen hundred men of the 42nd Mississippi, 2nd Mississippi, and 55th North Carolina on line, the six hundred-strong 11th Mississippi having been left in the rear as division train guards. Heth had thus committed thirty-five hundred Rebels to the assault on McPherson's Ridge; he had yet to send any message back to A. P. Hill at his Cashtown headquarters, several miles distant.

The Virginian had provided sufficient artillery support for the attack, having at hand the four batteries belonging to the battalion of Major William J. "Willie" Pegram, one of the Confederacy's premiere gunners. By the time Archer and Davis had their men shifted from column to line, Pegram had nineteen guns in position. When Calef opened fire on Davis's Brigade, Pegram ordered the two nearest batteries, Captain Edward Marye's Fredericksburg (Virginia) Artillery and Lieutenant Andrew Johnston's Crenshaw (Virginia) Artillery, to return fire, answering the four of Calef's guns that could bear with twice their number. "The demoniac 'whir-r-r' of the rifled shot, the 'ping' of the bursting shell and the wicked 'zip' of the bullet, as it hurried by filled the air," Calef observed. Undaunted, he ordered his two available sections to fire slowly and develop the full Confederate strength.

Going into battle in the midst of an artillery duel was nothing new for the Alabama and Tennessee troops of Archer's Brigade, but they soon ran into a different kind of trouble—the terrain around Willoughby Run. The creek subtly changed direction between the two ridges, angling first south, then east, then south again, and a particularly marshy piece of ground existed just north of the Herbst farm house. As a result, the 1st Tennessee (which had to traverse the swampy area) fell behind the brigade's left wing, while the 13th Alabama drifted off toward the south. Appearing "very much exhausted with fatigue," Archer himself (on foot, not on horseback) headed quickly for that end of the line, effectively isolating the 5th Alabama Battalion, 14th Tennessee, and 7th Tennessee just as they entered McPherson's Woods. Opposed only by the cavalry brigade on McPherson's Ridge, this would not have been a critical misstep, but as he attempted to realign his two straying regiments Archer had his first intimation that more Yankees were closer than either he or Heth had believed. Captain James A. Hall's 2nd Maine Light Artillery, according to Private R. T. Mockbee of the 14th Tennessee, "dashed out and took position on the ridge and opened fire," just as the Volunteer State soldiers "raised a yell and charged across Willoughby Run. . . ."

Separated from his left wing by several hundred yards, Archer must have remembered his brigade's costly disorganization at Chancellorsville, but there would only have been moments left for such reflection as nearly two thousand Yankee infantrymen suddenly crashed into his dispersed line, and the shout went up among the veterans, "That's no militia, that's the Iron Brigade!"

CHAPTER 3

Tell the General That We Will Hold

Approaching his twenty-fifth birthday as he neared the Pennsylvania border, Lieutenant Colonel Rufus R. Dawes of the 6th Wisconsin viewed the unfolding campaign with the skeptical eye of a seasoned veteran. He had shared these observations with his hometown sweetheart, Mary Gates. As the Iron Brigade, to which his regiment belonged, tramped past Centreville, Dawes spoke of "our annual visit to Bull Run," but hoped to "miss our annual drubbing." "Our army is in a great hurry for something," he wrote on June 15, and the successive long marches left the entire 1st Division, I Corps, "tired, sore, sleepy, hungry, dusty, and dirty as pigs." By June 18 word had reached the troops that Lee had crossed the Potomac, and "We are hurrying to the rescue of Pennsylvania and Maryland as I never knew the Army of the Potomac to hurry before." A week later, Dawes had become more cynical: "General Hooker shows no disposition to press the enemy so long as he confines his attention to the Pennsylvania Dutchmen and leaves Washington alone." Even so, he was not prepared for "Fighting Joe's" ouster, confiding to Mary on June 30 that "General Meade as commander of the army was a surprise. Meade lacked the martial bearing and presence of Hooker." The day before Gettysburg, Dawes had the same sense of something brewing that his soldiers felt: "The rebel stealing parties are running away ahead of us and I presume the rebel army is concentrating to give us battle."

On the morning of July 1, camped about eight miles from Gettysburg, Dawes paused after breakfast to write Mary another letter when the order came: "Pack up, be ready to march immediately." Scrawling, "I will finish this letter the first chance I get," Dawes began barking commands to get the 6th Wisconsin prepared to move out. Just the fact that the orders had come so early—his watch read 7:30 A.M.— suggested something was afoot, for the midwesterners had been scheduled for at least another hour of rest before resuming their trek north in pursuit of Lee's army. Brigadier General James Wadsworth's 1st Division had led the I Corps march yesterday, and it was normally Reynolds's practice to have his divisions alternate in the advance. Dawes's brigade commander, Brigadier General Solomon Meredith, had already told him that the 3rd Division under Major General Abner Doubleday would march past their bivouac on Marsh Creek before it would be time to have his companies formed up. The change in plans, therefore, was significant.

What neither Dawes nor his men knew was that Reynolds had ridden ahead to assess the situation around Gettysburg personally. Because he thought there was a good chance the cavalry would soon become embroiled in a fight, Reynolds decided he could not afford the time for Wadsworth's men to sit by the road as the next division leap-frogged past, so the corps commander told Double-day at 6:00 A.M. that he would take the 1st Division ahead with him. "He then instructed me to draw in pickets, assemble the artillery and the remainder of the corps, and join him as soon as possible," Doubleday recalled. "Having given these orders he rode off . . . and I never saw him again."

Wadsworth had his brigades in motion by 8:00 A.M., while Doubleday concerned himself with bringing along his own division and that of Brigadier General John C. Robinson. Prudence rather than urgency attached itself to all of these orders; Reynolds did not *know* that Buford had been attacked, but he was quite aware—as Dawes had told Mary—that his soldiers had spent the past two weeks "trudging along all day," often "in a soaking rain, getting as wet as a drowned rat, taking supper on hard tack and salt pork, and then wrapping up in a wet woolen blanket. . . ." If there was battle ahead, he wanted his men in good condition for the fight, so Wadsworth's division set off no faster than its usual pace, and Doubleday did not have his brigades on the Millerstown road until 9:30 A.M. The ninety-minute interval appeared inconsequential.

Like Heth's command, Wadsworth's division was something of an oddity, led by three of the oldest generals in the army, none of whom was a professional soldier. James Wadsworth, a white-maned but fit fifty-six-year-old New Yorker, was a wealthy landowner and prominent Republican politician when the war started. His fervor and his political connections allowed him to jump from general's aide-de-camp at Bull Run to brigadier general one month later. He had actually been a gubernatorial candidate in the fall of 1862, losing the race primarily because he would not go home to campaign; his consolation prize turned out to be George Meade's old division. While some West Pointers disparaged him as the prototypical "political general"— Doubleday said "he had little or no military skill, and did not profess to have any"—Wadsworth earned the respect of his men by paying close attention to their needs. He checked rations, quizzed his surgeons, and on the march into Pennsylvania took the footwear from civilians alongside the road to provide for soldiers whose shoes had worn out. The troops never forgot the sight, during the Chancellorsville campaign, of Wadsworth swimming his horse across the Rappahannock while they rode in the boats.

Massachusetts-born, fifty-nine-year-old Lysander Cutler had moved to Dexter, Maine, in 1828, going into the textile business. In 1835 he became one of the charter organizers of the Dexter Rifles, and two years later won election as colonel of the 9th Maine Militia. When the Panic of 1857 destroyed his fortune, Cutler moved to Milwaukee, becoming a grain broker and the city's fish inspector, a post he gave up in 1861 to become colonel of the 6th Wisconsin. A strong disciplinarian who quickly became battle-hardened in the Iron Brigade, one Pennsylvania officer characterized him as "one of those officers who always had his troops ready, and in the morning moved out at the designated time, breakfast or no breakfast." A promotion to brigadier general in late November 1862, caused Cutler to be transferred to the 1st Division's 2nd Brigade, composed of the 76th, 84th (usually known as the 14th Brooklyn), 95th, and 147th New York, as well as the 56th Pennsylvania and the 7th Indiana. With the exception of the 147th New York, Cutler's regiments had all seen at least one year's service. Marching up Emmittsburg Road that morning the brigade left behind the 434-man 7th Indiana as wagon guards, allowing Cutler to take only 1,583 men into battle.

Trailing Cutler's five regiments came the much-heralded Iron Brigade, composed of the 19th Indiana, 24th Michigan, and 2nd, 6th, and 7th Wisconsin—the only exclusively midwestern brigade in the Army of the Potomac, and damn proud of that fact and its nearly unparalleled fighting record. At the head of these 1,829 veterans rode fifty-three-year-old Brigadier General Solomon "Long Sol" Meredith, six feet, seven inches of grit, political ambition, and absolutely no military sense whatever. Born a North Carolina Quaker, as a young man Meredith walked across Tennessee and Kentucky to reach Indiana, where he threw himself into politics, eventually becoming a Republican state legislator, U. S. Marshall, and close friend of Governor Oliver P. Morton. That friendship landed him the colonelcy of the 19th Indiana, where the best one soldier could find to say about him was that "Colonel Meredith talks right, acts right, and in fact does the very best that he knows how. I think he means well." When it was rumored that he might be promoted, even after missing the battle of Antietam, the

Brigadier General Solomon Meredith. *(Library of Congress)*

regimental surgeon wrote, "If he is not [promoted], there will soon be a petition signed by the whole Regt. for him to resign." Many of the Indiana soldiers apparently supported his promotion quite actively, on the assumption that he would then be transferred to another unit. To their horror, he inherited command of the Iron Brigade instead. At Fredericksburg, Doubleday had relieved him from command for failing to carry out his order; at Chancellorsville he crossed the Rappahannock only after his regiments had taken several dozen casualties to establish their bridgehead. In short, paraphrasing Clifford Dowdey about Heth's Division, one of the best brigades in the army had been given an incompetent leader, which had caused a better man to be transferred out, and both men were fighting under the army's oldest division commander whose chief military qualification was that he was not the governor of New York. Still, this was a solid division, even if only half the size of Heth's, and if given a chance it would conquer proudly or die in the attempt.

Reynolds spurred his horse ahead of Wadsworth's division, anxious to reach Buford and discover the situation at Gettysburg. He knew that Meade was unsure precisely how to respond to Lee's invasion, and that the army commander's visceral preference was to stake out some position on strong ground and hope that the Rebels would oblige him by attacking. Meade had already tentatively examined such terrain at Pipe Creek, to the south, but that would actually involve what appeared to be a retreat by the Army of the Potomac before it had even risked a battle, something the new commander might not be able to survive politically. Reynolds, with control of three corps, had the practical authority to commit the entire army to battle simply by concentrating his own divisions, and he knew Meade trusted his judgment. With a road configuration that would naturally induce both armies to concentrate there Gettysburg might be the right place, but Reynolds realized that he had to be sure.

The Pennsylvanian undoubtedly also had other matters on his mind that morning, the same sort of thoughts that haunted generals as much as privates when they contemplated the risks of battle. Beneath his uniform blouse Reynolds wore a gold ring, shaped like two clasped hands, hanging from a chain around his neck. He had never shown Wadsworth, Doubleday, Meade, or Buford that ring, inscribed "Dear Kate" for Katherine Hewitt, the woman he intended to marry. Before Lee had commenced his invasion, he and Kate had made a date in Philadelphia for mid-July, when Reynolds would finally meet her parents.

Reynolds was a front-line general who had never learned how to stand back in safety while men were dying in the ranks. He now needed to see the ground himself, as much as he trusted Buford's eye, before he would make a decision. As he turned off Emmitsburg Road at the Condori farm, Reynolds paused to look east at the Round Tops,

Cemetery Ridge, Cemetery Hill, and Culp's Hill, realizing that here stood a potentially impregnable position, if only the army could be concentrated swiftly enough. He found Buford in the seminary cupola minutes after 10:00 A.M., observing Heth's Division on Herr Ridge as Archer assembled his troops for the attack, and asked, "What goes, John?" Buford swore—"The Devil's to pay!"—but when Reynolds asked if his troopers could hold out until Wadsworth arrived, he said with quiet confidence, "I reckon so."

Requiring only minutes to assess the situation and see what Buford had seen, Reynolds sent a courier to Major General Oliver Otis Howard, the XI Corps commander, urging him to hurry toward Gettysburg. To Meade he dispatched a staff officer with a report making it clear that the Army of the Potomac would fight out the issue right here if the Rebels were willing: "Tell the General that we will hold the heights to the south of the town, and that I will barricade the town if necessary." Another messenger galloped back to get the I Corps moving at the double-quick.

The responsibilities of high command executed, Reynolds turned his attention to the immediate tactical situation. Heading back to the Codori farm to await Wadsworth's arrival, he sent his escort to start removing fences that might impede the cross-country movement of the lead brigade. As Cutler's regiments arrived, staffers shouted that "the rebs were thicker than blackberries ahead," and led them across the fields over Seminary Ridge toward McPherson's. Captain Hall's 2nd Maine Light Artillery initially followed, but an officer soon appeared with orders for the cannoneer to report in person to his corps commander.

Reynolds, now accompanied by Wadsworth, met Hall where Chambersburg Pike crossed McPherson's Ridge, running past the Edward McPherson's farm. Reynolds had already decided that the point of greatest danger lay immediately north of Chambersburg Pike, where only

Present-day photo looking west from McPherson's Ridge to McPherson's barn. Note how slight the ridge appears from this position.

about two to three hundred dismounted troopers from Devin's brigade held the ground in front of McPherson's Ridge. Pointing out Pegram's artillery on the other side of Willoughby Run, Reynolds said, "Put your battery on this ridge to engage those guns of the enemy." It was a dangerously exposed position, and Hall could already count at least ten Confederate guns firing. Reynolds understood the captain's apprehension, and told Wadsworth to "move a strong infantry support immediately to Hall's right, for he is my defender until I can get the troops now coming up into line." To Hall the corps commander said, "I desire you to damage the artillery to the greatest possible extent, and to keep their fire from our infantry until they are well deployed," after which he promised, "I will retire you somewhat as you are too far advanced for the general line."

Cutler's brigade meanwhile had been moving steadily north in through the fold between McPherson's and Seminary Ridges, concealed from the enemy's view. When they reached Chambersburg Pike, Reynolds rode up with deployment orders. He instructed Cutler to take his two leading regiments—the 76th New York and 56th Pennsylvania (627 men in all)—north of the road and past the railroad cut that ran parallel to it. At that point they would turn west, crest McPherson's Ridge, and move forward to relieve the cavalry and secure Hall's right flank. Colonel Edward Fowler was to lead his own 14th Brooklyn and the 95th New York (559 troops) onto McPherson's Ridge just south of the pike, taking up a position on Hall's left between McPherson's Farm and the woods. Unfortunately, everyone forgot about Cutler's greenest regiment, Lieutenant Colonel Francis Miller's 147th New York, which received no orders at all as the rest of the brigade marched off in different directions. Miller moved his 380 men under the cover of McPherson's stone barn, just south of Chambersburg Pike, and hurried off to find anyone who could tell him what to do. About that time, Hall's battery galloped over the ridge, unlimbered, and started to fire.

Lieutenant Colonel Kress, no longer looking for shoes, had in the interim found Wadsworth, and pointed out to him that sending Cutler north was all well and good, but that Archer's Brigade had started moving down Herr Ridge toward Willoughby Run. Even though Fowler's 14th Brooklyn had noticed the attack and turned to fire into Archer's flank, only a few hundred thoroughly exhausted cavalrymen stood between the Alabama–Tennessee brigade and McPherson's Ridge. Wadsworth sent Kress to fetch the Iron Brigade, also moving up along the eastern slope of McPherson's Ridge. The staffer located Colonel Lucius Fairchild, whose 2nd Wisconsin marched in the lead, but "Long Sol" Meredith was nowhere to be found. On his own initiative, Kress ordered Fairchild to "form his regiment forward into line, double-quick, saying that he would find the enemy in his immediate front as soon as he could form." As Fairchild's troops crossed the ridge, Kress repeated the same orders to the officers commanding the 7th Wisconsin, 24th Michigan, and 19th Indiana. Colonel

Henry Morrow of the 24th Michigan tried to halt long enough for his men to load their weapons, but Kress insisted that there was no time to spare, and ordered him "to move forward immediately without loading, which I did." Kress halted Dawes's 6th Wisconsin in place to become the division's only reserve.

At McPherson's Ridge the Iron Brigade proved what crack troops could do without a brigade commander. Fairchild's 2nd Wisconsin poured over the ridge, paused long enough only for the officers to dismount, and charged. The 7th and 14th Tennessee, on Archer's left flank, managed to get off what one Wisconsin soldier characterized as a "murderous volley" that killed Lieutenant Colonel George Stevens and severely wounded Colonel Fairchild. Major John Mansfield assumed command with his regiment just fifty yards away from the Confederate line, and led them in. Colonel William Robinson's 7th Wisconsin had meanwhile crested the ridge, and looking down into the smoke-swathed ravine he decided to wait for the 24th Michigan and 19th Indiana to join him for a concerted attack. This decision sealed Archer's fate.

Archer's right wing, the 13th Alabama and 1st Tennessee, had kept pushing forward, out of the creekbed and up the slope despite Fairchild's attack, meeting the 19th Indiana just as the Hoosiers crossed the ridge. Private W. H. Bird of the 13th Alabama remembered his shock when "all of a sudden a heavy line of battle rose up out of the wheat, and poured a volley into our ranks. . . ." Bird's comrades "wavered, and they charged us, and we fell back to the ravine again." It was a mutual surprise; Colonel Samuel Williams reported that his men had opened fire spontaneously and charged without orders. To Williams's left the 24th Michigan discovered that it had entered the fray on Archer's flank, and with the killer instinct of elite soldiers, the regiment lapped around the 13th Alabama's left.

The melee was brutal. Captain Robert K. Beecham of the 2nd Wisconsin caught its essence: "the unadorned long-drawn-out line of ragged, dirty blue against the long-drawn-out line of dirty, ragged butternut, with no 'pomp of war' about it, and no show or style. . . ." Caught in a vise, Archer's Brigade dissolved. Private Bird felt like "there were 20,000 Yanks down in among us hallowing surrender," and on the other end of the line Major Mansfield reported that "the line of the enemy in our immediate front"—the 7th Tennessee—"yielded." The chaplain of the 47th Virginia thought that barely "one-third of the brigade fled back upon the line being formed by Brockenbrough's Virginians." Archer's four regiments and one battalion had taken at least 373 casualties (including between seventy-five and one hundred prisoners), and its organization was so shattered that Heth immediately decided to pull it out of the fight.

Among those who failed to elude the Federals was Archer himself. Staggering with fever and exhaustion, the brigade commander had picked his way through the underbrush and nearly reached Willoughby Run, when Private Patrick Mahoney of the 2nd Wisconsin caught him. (Mahoney, killed later that day, would receive a posthumous Medal of Honor for this exploit.) Being escorted into captivity, Archer by chance met Doubleday—a friend from his prewar days—and the Union officer exclaimed, "Good morning, Archer! How are you? I am glad to see you!"

"Well, I am *not* glad to see *you* by a ---- sight," the enraged Marylander replied.

Yet victory had also cost the Federals dearly. From a vantage point far too close to leading troops, Reynolds had been urging the 2nd Wisconsin into its initial head-long charge, shouting, "Forward men, forward for God's sake, and drive those fellows out of the woods." He had turned back to see if the rest of the Iron Brigade had followed, when a bullet struck the base of his skull. There were no last words for the general; he toppled from his horse, dead before he hit the earth. The commander who had set three corps in motion and hazarded the entire Army of the

Major General John F. Reynolds.
(Library of Congress)

**John Reynold's monument
at Gettysburg.**

Potomac in a fight to the death at Gettysburg would never know the outcome of his decision. Moreover, that Gamble's line had held by the slimmest of margins, might not matter; north of Chambersburg Pike, Cutler's brigade faced destruction in detail.

CHAPTER 4

BALLS WHISTLED ROUND OUR HEADS LIKE HAIL

ONE WEEK EARLIER, THE 2ND MISSISSIPPI had forded the Potomac River and crossed the old battlefield west of Antietam Creek, where the regiment had taken 154 casualties in the cornfield north of Sharpsburg. Both Colonel John M. Stone and Major John A. Blair had been wounded there, and the men paid somber attention as they passed through. "Much sign of the conflict is visible," noted twenty-three-year-old George Bynum of Company A. He commented in his diary about "the low mounds which cover the bones of those who fell, the furrowed ground, and scarred trees," and ended the entry with the recollection: "I saw the ground over which we charged on that memorable occasion and the very spot where I was wounded." Captured and paroled a few days later, Bynum had been promoted to corporal the following month. He was one of five brothers who served in Company A; by Gettysburg, two had already been discharged, but nineteen-year-old Nathaniel remained in the ranks as a private, while twenty-one-year-old Turner had risen to second sergeant.

Ten months earlier both the 2nd and 11th Mississippi had been in the brigade of Evander M. Law in John Bell Hood's division, veterans surrounded by veterans. Now, however, these two regiments had been brigaded with the green 42nd Mississippi and 55th North Carolina, all placed under the equally unseasoned Brigadier General Joseph R. Davis.

Marching toward Gettysburg the 11th Mississippi had been detailed as wagon guard, so when Heth ordered Davis to place his brigade in line of battle north of Chambersburg Pike, Davis placed his only veterans (and smallest regiment at 492 men), the 2nd Mississippi, in the center. Private Samuel Hankins, Company E, recalled that Colonel Stone "came down the line, stopping in front of each company and giving instructions." When he reached Company E, the six-foot-tall, thirty-three-year-old regimental commander said calmly, "Men, clean out your guns, load, and be ready. We are going to have it!"

On the right end of the brigade line, closest to Chambersburg Pike and nearly straddling the embankment on the unfinished railroad cut running almost parallel to the main road, Davis had deployed Colonel Hugh R. Miller's 42nd Mississippi, 575 strong. Miller, a fifty-one-year-old South Carolinian who had moved to Mississippi in 1840, had as his primary military qualifications the fact that he was circuit court judge, state legislator, and delegate to Mississippi's secession convention. To the far left marched the 55th North Carolina, 640 troops commanded by Colonel John K. Connally, a twenty-three-year-old Tennessee transplant who had become a Carolina lawyer after attending (but not graduating from) the U. S. Naval Academy. General Dorsey Pender considered Connally "a most conceited fellow." About Davis, the neophyte brigadier, there is a surprising dearth of comment in Confederate veterans' reminiscences, as if the less said the better. The soldiers of the 42nd Mississippi and 55th North Carolina would prove over the next two years as brave (and eventually as skilled) as any of Lee's veterans, but this day, leavened only by Stone's 2nd Mississippi, they were going to pass through hell for their initiation.

The early moments of Davis's Brigade's advance went well enough, primarily because Devin's brigade—spread even more thinly than Gamble's—had only a few pickets with which to offer any resistance. Lieutenant J. B.

Gambrell, commanding Stone's skirmish line, "kept pressing back that of the enemy," one soldier recalled, and Sergeant Augustus Vairin remembered "going over many plank fences—hard work for me, who was gaulded [sic] badly by the march." Private Hankins described entering the fields of McPherson's Farm, covered with wheat ready for harvest," and looking east at McPherson's Ridge, "up a slope to the edge of a line of timber." South of the pike, "only a short distance could be seen on account of hills," but that area was the responsibility of the 42nd Mississippi.

After moving forward nearly one mile, however, Miller's 42nd Missisippi began to lag behind. Captain Hall's 2nd Maine Battery had opened fire on the Confederate artillery on Herr Ridge from his hilltop position near McPherson's barn. Though his fire, at thirteen hundred yards distance, had little effect on the Rebel guns, except to make Pegram

A present-day photo looking east up McPherson's Ridge between the barn and the woods toward the Federal artillery position of the New York Light Artillery.

move two pieces to better positions, it drew Colonel Miller's attention quickly enough. The 42nd Mississippi (or at least several companies) pivoted to the right to attack the offending battery; with green troops this maneuver took extra time. Hall reported that twenty-five minutes passed before "a column of the enemy's infantry charged up a ravine on our right flank within sixty yards of my right piece, when they commenced shooting down my horses and wounding my men." The Maine gunners hastily loaded four cannon with canister, swung the trails around "and broke the charge of the enemy. . . ." Miller's Mississippians, shocked at first blood, scampered back into the cover of the railroad cut, while Hall wondered exactly what had happened to the regiments of Cutler's brigade that were supposed to secure his right flank.

As Hall was repulsing that attack, Colonel Francis Miller had finally sorted out where the 380 men of his 147th New York were supposed to be headed. Cutler's original intention had been for the 147th to accompany the 56th Pennsylvania and 76th New York across Chambersburg Pike behind Seminary Ridge, over the railroad cut, and then turn west to cross McPherson's Ridge and come up even with Hall's battery. Having been separated from the other two regiments, the best the 147th could now do was to leave the shelter of McPherson's barn and strike directly north across the pike, hoping to join the other regiments as they came down off the ridge and into the wheatfield. Colonel Miller shouted the order, "By the left flank, guide center!" as his companies passed over the railroad cut, intending to wheel his regiment to the left and then link up with the 56th Pennsylvania. Unfortunately, due to what Colonel William J. Hoffmann of the 56th Pennsylvania called "the rail fence and a dense growth of bushes along its line," neither regiment could see the other, and the New Yorkers did not realize that a diagonal gap of at least 150 yards separated them from the Pennsylvanians they sought.

What the New Yorkers *did* see was the 42nd Mississippi, now sending out a company of skirmishers to pick off the horses and gunners of Hall's battery. Such a tactic was far more difficult for the artillerymen to defend against than the charge of an entire regiment. Against a widely dispersed skirmish line canister became ineffective, while sharpshooters could stand off at relatively safe range and pick their targets. "To resist them," Abner Doubleday later remarked, "would be very much like fighting mosquitoes with musket-balls." Not having witnessed the 147th New York cross the pike, Hall reported that "feeling that if the position was too advanced for infantry it was equally so for artillery, I ordered the battery to retire by sections, although having no order to do so." So many horses were killed in the sniping that the cannoneers had to drag one gun back by hand, and abandon another. "It was hellish," Hall said in 1871, "to stop and hold them and hold my men to attempt to rescue [the last gun] was madness on my part and I moved to the rear."

By the time the Maine battery made it east of Seminary Ridge, Hall had five guns, but only enough horses and artillerymen to fight three of his six-inch rifles. There the exhausted captain encountered General Wadsworth, and promptly forgot about the difference between their respective ranks to deliver a blistering dissertation on the "cowardly" decision to leave his last piece for the Mississippians. Wadsworth understood the ordeal Hall had just come through, but he was not about to be hectored by a battery commander in the middle of a battle he appeared to be losing. "Get your guns back to some point to cover the retiring of these troops," he ordered. Hall allowed that his current vantage point on Seminary Ridge would serve, to which the general responded, "Oh no, go beyond the town for we cannot hold this line." Hall balked, insisting that something be done to save his sixth gun, to which the division commander tersely replied, "Lose no time in getting your guns into position to cover the

An engraving depicting part of the battle on the McPherson farm on July 1, 1863. Confederate infantrymen storm the stone barn held by soldiers from Pennsylvania.

Present-day photo looking out of McPherson's woods toward McPherson's barn with Chambersburg Pike in background, land that was hard fought for on the first day of the battle of Gettysburg.

retreat," and moved off, thinking the matter concluded. Unrepentant, Hall moved his battery back according to orders, but left behind a sergeant with a detail of five men with the impossible task of sneaking back to recover the last cannon.

Back at the site of Hall's discomfiture, Mississippians *had* seen the New Yorkers, and the considerably larger Confederate regiment immediately opened fire. "Men dropped dead and the wounded men went to the rear before they had emptied their muskets," observed Lieutenant J. Volney Pierce, Company G, 147th New York, while Private Francis Pease of Company F noted a week later that "balls whistled round our heads like hail. The men very soon began to fall very fast and many wounded." Gamely the New Yorkers moved toward the crest of the ridge, where Colonel Miller ordered them to lie down and fire back.

Meanwhile, the rest of Cutler's brigade had also found the enemy. The 56th Pennsylvania and 76th New York crested McPherson's Ridge "marching by the flank," and encountered almost immediate fire from the skirmish lines of the 2nd Mississippi and 55th North Carolina. The "head-on" clash that ensued appears to have been a mutual surprise. Captain John Cook of the 76th New York reported that the Rebels "were lying down concealed from view in a wheat-field," while Private Hankins remembered that the Yankees were "in the wheat . . . lying down" until the 2nd Mississippi approached "up the slope to within good shot of their line, [when] they jumped to their feet and opened fire on us." At point-blank range, as historian Scott Hartwig observes, "it was stand-up fighting of the bloodiest nature." The 56th Pennsylvania lost seventy-nine men killed and wounded in twenty minutes, and the 76th New York took 169 casualties, including its commanding officer, Major Andrew Grover. Among the dozens of Rebels hit by return fire were Colonels Stone and Connally.

What defeated the Yankees in twenty minutes time was

Major Andrew Grover.
(Library of Congress)

weight of numbers. Cutler had 627 men in his two regiments; Davis, with 1,132, had nearly twice as many. Inexperienced as he was, Davis knew to order the 55th North Carolina to wheel around Cutler's right flank for a decisive blow. His New Yorkers and Pennsylvanians, Cutler insisted, "fought as only brave men can fight," and no shame attached itself to the fact that when Wadsworth sent the belated order to retreat, the retrograde was more rapid than orderly. As they reached the relative safety of the east side of Seminary Ridge, Cutler set about reorganizing the fewer than four hundred men remaining under his immediate control, telling them, "It was just like cockfighting today. We fight a little and run a little."

What Cutler did not realize was that Wadsworth's retreat order had reached Colonel Miller but never made it to his men of the 147th New York. Miller took a bullet in the throat, and his horse bolted before he could pass the word to Major George Harney. Amid the smoke, Harney and his officers mistook a Confederate movement glimpsed through the billowing clouds for a retreat, and therefore attempted to hold their ground. Unfortunately, this movement was no retreat, but the 2nd Mississippi and 55th North Carolina maneuvering around to come in on the New Yorker's exposed right flank. The Mississippians were now in the competent hands of Major Blair, while the North Carolinians had actually profited from Connally's loss, since command devolved on Major Alfred H. Belo, an infinitely more competent officer.

Staying as low as possible, the New Yorkers found themselves suddenly pressed on three sides by overwhelming numbers. Captain Nathaniel Wright crawled about the ground shouting "give them h___," and Lieutenant Pierce remembered that his comrades dropped "like autumn leaves, the air was full of lead." Wounded soldiers had to be piled into the railroad cut because they could not be evacuated from the field. Completely isolated, Harney called his six surviving officers together to discuss their predicament. Without orders, only two courses appeared possible: surrender to save the lives of as many men as possible, or fight it out to the death. Surrender had just been ruled out by a unanimous negative when Lieutenant Timothy Ellsworth of Wadsworth's staff rode through the storm of lead, "his coal-black hair pressing his horse's mane," to deliver the retreat order. Waiting only long enough to advise his troops to shuck all their equipment but rifles and cartridge boxes, Harney called out, "In retreat, double-quick, run!"

Color Sergeant William Wyburn, though shot through the body and almost left for dead, managed to stagger back across Chambersburg Pike with the regimental colors. That heroic run prompted an apology from Cutler, who had been haranguing the surviving officers about losing their flag, but represented only the hollowest of moral victories for the 147th New York. Cutler's official report summarized the situation all too accurately: "The loss of this gallant regiment was fearful at this point, being 2 officers killed and 10 wounded, 42 men killed and 153 wounded—207 out of 380 men and officers within half an hour." Many of the wounded in the railroad cut were hit again when a company of the 2nd Mississippi clambered down into the west end of the ditch and opened fire. That afternoon the remaining troops were consolidated into two companies.

The Federal position north of Chambersburg Pike had collapsed. The victorious Mississippians and North Carolinians, though intermixed and disorganized themselves, were threatening to sweep down McPherson's Ridge, roll up the last two regiments of Cutler's brigade, and catch the Iron Brigade before it could disentangle itself from the boggy ground around Willoughby Run.

CHAPTER 5

AS ONLY BRAVE MEN CAN FIGHT

BETWEEN HALL'S BATTERY ON CHAMBERSBURG PIKE and McPherson's Woods, where Archer's troops and the Iron Brigade were struggling for control of Willoughby Run, were the other two regiments of Cutler's brigade. Ostensibly, the 14th Brooklyn and 95th New York, under command of Colonel Edward Fowler of the 14th, had been assigned to protect the Maine artillerymen's exposed left flank, but these New Yorkers found themselves in a strange no-man's land between different fights. Initially, when Archer's Rebels had crossed the creek, Fowler's men had been able to pour fire into their flank, but now the 2nd Wisconsin and the 7th Tennessee were fighting it out in the woods, too intermingled for the New Yorker's to fire safely. On Fowler's right, the structures of McPherson's Farm kept Colonel George Biddle's 95th New York from participating in—or even seeing—the clash between the 147th New York and the 42nd Mississippi. Other than the sounds of firing north of the pike, the first notice that Fowler's two regiments received of the disaster unfolding there occurred when Mississippi skirmishers came over McPherson's Ridge and seized Hall's abandoned gun.

Without either orders or an enemy to his front, Fowler barked out the command for both regiments "to march in retreat until on a line with the enemy, and then changed front perpendicular to face them. . . ." As the New Yorkers were executing this maneuver, unexpected assistance suddenly arrived. Sensing disaster in the making, General Doubleday (although still unaware that Reynolds had been killed and he was now acting corps commander) had sought out Wadsworth's only remaining reserve, Colonel Dawes's 6th Wisconsin, augmented by the men earlier detailed as the brigade guard. The Iron Brigade's commander, General Meredith, had just ridden up to order Dawes's men into the fray along Willoughby Creek, but Doubleday overrode him, shouting for the Wisconsin regiment to double-quick toward Chambersburg Pike, where the 56th Pennsylvania and 76th New York were fleeing back across Seminary Ridge.

The 6th Wisconsin's left encountered the right wing of the 95th New York as it swung around on Fowler's orders. The result of this meeting was an impromptu three-regiment line *en echelon*, with the 6th Wisconsin slightly ahead and the 14th Brooklyn far enough behind that Dawes did not at first realize Fowler's regiment was present. No one was in overall command of this force. Fowler had made the decision to charge into the Rebels as soon as his two regiments were on line, but Colonel George H. Biddle of the 95th New York had gone down, and his successor, Major Edward Pye, apparently did not know the plan.

Dawes, having "reached a fence on the Chambersburg turnpike, about 40 rods from the line of the enemy," instantly realized the enormity of the crisis, as he beheld Davis's Mississippians and North Carolinians "pressing rapidly in pursuit of our retreating line, threatening the rear of the First Brigade (Meredith's Iron Brigade). . . ." Halting his men, he ordered them to fire by file, in an attempt to distract the Rebels's attention toward their own flank. Private Albert Young said later that "the Johnnies were so intent upon following their advantage that they did not for some time discover what was happening on their right," but then abruptly "jumped into an old railroad cut which is immediately in front of them and here about five feet deep and opened up on us." Young wrote with the advantage of hindsight; no one in Dawes's regiment had any idea before that moment that the railroad cut existed, and one Wisconsin soldier said simply, "Their whole line disappeared as if swallowed up by the earth." Moments later, however, Davis's Brigade opened a counterfire that Dawes would describe as "murderous." Dawes knew that his regiment could neither stay where it was nor retreat. As his men started to fall, he ran across to the 95th New York and found Major Pye. "Let's go for them, Major!" he called over the din of the firing. Pye may not have understood Fowler's intent, but he could read the tactical situation as clearly as Dawes; he answered immediately, "We're with you!"

"Forward charge! Align on the Colors! Align on the Colors!" Dawes bellowed. "I did not hear Col. Dawes command to charge," wrote Lieutenant Lloyd G. Harris, commanding the Iron Brigade guard (neither, doubtless, did hundreds of others), "but I saw the colors moving forward; that was enough."

When the bulk of the 2nd Mississippi and 55th North Carolina had been ordered into the railroad cut, a number of men realized that the ditch could be a death trap or a prison pen instead of a shelter. Augustus Vairin remembered that "our men thought [it] would prove a good breastwork but it was too deep & in changing front the men were tangled up & confused." Samuel Hankins, who had been shot in the foot, discovered with four other wounded Mississippians that "our place of 'safety' was very much exposed, as shot and shell were tearing up the earth all about us." The source of this order was not the acting regimental commander's. Major Belo had just had a quick conference with Major Blair (perhaps five minutes before Dawes and Pye met on the other side of the line). Belo remarked that "It occurred to me at this moment that our brigade, being flushed with victory, should charge" the 6th Wisconsin and the two New York outfits "at once before they could form in line of battle." He had just convinced

Blair to have the 2nd Mississippi join in the attack when "we received the command to retire through the cut."

The order came from General Davis, whose inexperience cost his troops dearly. In attempting to justify his decision, the Mississippi brigadier characterized the 6th Wisconsin's initial appearance thus: "a heavy force was observed moving rapidly toward our right, and soon after opened a heavy fire on our right flank and rear. In this critical condition, I gave the order to retire. . . ." Davis appears to have been buffaloed by his own brigade's success, for the numbers suggested that Major Blair was more nearly right when he bemoaned the fact that the withdrawal cost the chance to "capture Gettysburg without further difficulty . . . and end the war right there." Even allowing for casualties in the earlier fighting and men temporarily dislocated in the confusion of the fight, Davis's Brigade had at least thirteen to fifteen hundred Rebels available; the 6th Wisconsin, Iron Brigade guard, and the 95th New York could not have had more than seven hundred soldiers on line, and the 14th Brooklyn was—for the moment—too far back to be a consideration.

Momentum, however, shifts position capriciously on the battlefield, though rarely more rapidly than it did above Chambersburg Pike between 11:15–11:30 A.M. on July 1, 1863. The Rebels—"flushed with victory" as Belo put it— abruptly found a large, aggressive force pouring fire into their flank. The crisis of confidence that created was more in the mind of Joseph R. Davis than in those of his men, but when they were suddenly ordered to retreat everything fell apart. Some entered the railroad cut and discovered that the ditch was too deep and the banks too steep in many places to stand and return fire. Others climbed out over the northern embankment, but were then left essentially leaderless in the wheatfield beyond. In both cases, men lost track of their own companies, even their own regiments. Belo, Blair, and the other surviving officer worked as hard as possible to restore some semblance of organization;

unfortunately, that process would have required about ten minutes that neither the 6th Wisconsin nor the 95th New York planned to give them.

Despite the Confederate disarray, the Federals took heavy losses crossing the 175 yards that separated them from the railroad cut. Dawes estimated that his regiment lost 160 out of 344 men in fifteen minutes. Officers and colorbearers fell, and Dawes would write to Mary six days later: "May God save me and my men from any more such trials. I could tell a thousand stories of their heroism: One young man, Corporal James Kelly of company 'B,' shot through the breast, came staggering up to me before he fell and opening his shirt to show the wound, said, 'Colonel, won't you write to my folks that I died a soldier.'"

The colorbearer of the 2nd Mississippi, Sergeant William B. Murphy, had posted himself and his detail just outside the railroad cut, possibly to encourage his regiment to leave that dangerous ground. To the Federals his waving flag constituted the matador's cape before the lunging bull, and the fight for the 2nd Mississippi's flag took on a legendary aspect all its own in the middle of the greater battle. "We made a desperate struggle for our colors," Murphy wrote. "My color guards were all killed and wounded in less than five minutes, and also my colors were shot more than a dozen times, and the flagstaff was shot and splintered two or three more times." Leading the pack to seize that tattered flag was Corporal Francis A. Wallar, Company I, 6th Wisconsin, who recounted: "I started straight for it, as did lots of others." Wallar—"a large man"—tackled Murphy, threw him to the ground, and tore the banner from his hands. "Soon after I got the flag there were men from all of the companies there," Wallar admitted, but "I did take the flag out of the color-bearer's hand." He received the Medal of Honor for this exploit.

Dawes and most of the remaining men of the 6th Wisconsin (no more than 180 at this point) reached the edge of the embankment, while his adjutant took a party of

Present-day photo of the walls of the railroad cut at its deepest, where it was not really usable for defensive purposes.

Present-day photo of the railroad cut under the modern bridge over McPherson's Ridge. Note that the walls are less steep here and it looks more like a typical entrenchment.

twenty soldiers around to the right, actually dropping down into the ditch ready to deliver a bloody enfilade fire against the confused mass of Mississippians. "Throw down your muskets!" the Wisconsin troops yelled. Dawes ran up, saw "hundreds of rebels, whom I looked down upon in the railroad cut, which was, were I stood, four feet deep," and shouted, "Where is the colonel of this regiment?"

"Who are you?" Major Blair called back, aware that at any moment a murderous volley could shred his remaining men.

"I command this regiment. Surrender or I will fire."

Not trusting his voice, Blair handed Dawes his sword, and moments later at least 225 Mississippians—many of them wounded—began throwing down their rifles.

The remnants of Davis's Brigade (Heth used the word "shattered" in his official report) retreated more rapidly than Cutler's men had fallen back before them. Amazingly enough, all three Bynum brothers in Company A, 2nd Mississippi, made it out of the railroad cut (though Turner Bynum's luck would run out two days later when the Yankees captured him). D. J. Hill, another Mississippian who had not exited the cut when Blair gave up his sword, "was disgusted with the idea of surrendering," and avoided the prison pen through quick thinking. "I saw a bloody, muddy blanket lyin on the ground also two wounded men lying near me," Hill wrote in 1893. "I tumbled down by them and covered myself with the blanket. I then went to practicing all the manners and moaning that I thought would become a badly wounded and suffering man." In the confusion that followed the regiment's surrender, "I got out as soon as I thought it was safe to do so," and made his way back to Confederate lines.

Prisoners aside, dozens if not hundreds of wounded men from both armies died in the railroad cut before they could receive medical attention. Some had been left behind when the 147th New York ran for it; the rest probably belonged to the 2nd and 42nd Mississippi or the 55th North Carolina. In the temporary lull that set in for about an hour after this action, surgeons and litter bearers moved in to treat and evacuate as many of those still living as they could find. The dead had to be left where they had fallen.

The thin layers of earth thrown over those corpses by later Confederate burial parties were disturbed within days after the battle. Samuel Weaver, one of the men contracted to disinter, identify, and re-bury the dead in the Gettysburg National Cemetery, recorded that "the battle field had been overrun by thousands of sorrowing friends in search of lost ones, and many of the graves opened and but partially or carelessly closed." Undertakers commissioned by these mourners had left "particles of the bones and hair lying scattered around." Many bodies "were found in various stages of decomposition" and "could not be identified." Nonetheless, Gettysburg lawyer David Wills, who drew the assignment of supervising the entire operation and putting names with as many of the decaying corpses as possible, did his best to treat every recovered body—Yankee or Rebel—with respect. He noted that when he could not determine the identity of a particular soldier, he could almost always distinguish Northerners from Southerners because the Confederate rank and file had rarely worn either underwear or socks. Scrupulous lists were compiled of the belongings found with or near each fallen soldier, and later published in the hope that someone recognizing an artifact would be able to provide another grave with the appropriate name.

Inevitably, of course, some graves were never opened, some bodies never found. That was a truth all veterans lived with, like the aging former members of the 95th New York, who returned to the railroad cut on July 1, 1893, for the thirtieth anniversary of the battle. Some men simply disappeared without a trace, and could only be remembered in the absence of mortal remains. Yet the ground gives up most of its secrets eventually. In March 1996, workers at the Gettysburg Military Park discovered the skeleton of a soldier who died at the railroad cut on July 1, which had been hidden for 133 years. The *Houston Chronicle* reported in May 1997, that "a forensic pathologist with the Smithsonian's National Museum of Natural History determined the bones to be that of a white male between the ages of 20 and 25. . . . The anthropologist's report also cited a possible cause of death. The skull fracture patterns and the evidence of lead particles point to a gunshot wound to the head."

On July 1, 1997, with an honor guard provided by Civil War reenactors from the Iron Brigade and the 55th North Carolina, a detail from the 3rd U. S. Infantry (the "Old Guard" from Arlington National Cemetery) buried the last known—but ironically unknown—casualty from the bloody fight for the railroad cut.

CHAPTER 6

IT WAS THE INTENTION TO DEFEND
THE PLACE

ABNER DOUBLEDAY RECEIVED VERY LITTLE RESPECT from his peers, his soldiers, or even historians. Having just turned forty-four at the time of the battle of Gettysburg, the New Jersey native had been an artilleryman in the U. S. Army since graduating twenty-fourth in West Point's class of 1842. His initial claim to fame, that he fired the first Union shot at Fort Sumter, is still disputed; the tradition that he created baseball—despite its long-lived popularity—has been thoroughly debunked. Aside from those two associations, what remained was a rather pompous careerist, whose decisions on the battlefield were so deliberate that he earned the sobriquet "Forty-eight Hours," because the troops thought he moved as if there were that many hours in the day. Doubleday had never been singled out for promotion to high command, rising from brigade to division more through attrition and happenstance than the conscious intention of his superiors. George Meade thought so little of Doubleday's competence that, upon hearing of Reynolds's death, he immediately assigned Brigadier General John M. Newton (hardly a battlefield lion himself) to supercede the New Jersey native as acting I Corps commander. Even his own artillery chief, Colonel Charles Wainwright, considered Doubleday a "week reed" in whom he "had no confidence. . . ."

Not that Doubleday helped his own case. Infuriated at

65

the "base calumny" he considered responsible for Newton's appointment over him, he wrote "the longest battle report of the Union Army" to defend his actions at Gettysburg. Relieved of active field command (though he hung on in the army until 1873), he joined the cabal of officers determined in 1864 to prove that Chancellorsville had been lost despite the brilliance of Hooker and Gettysburg had been won despite the timidity and incompetence of George Meade. Even the end of the Civil War did not dampen Doubleday's ardor to improve his reputation, particularly at Meade's expense. Almost every single time he saw in print any praise of the army commander's conduct of the battle of Gettysburg, Doubleday published a rejoinder indicating that Meade had in fact planned to retreat, but had been drawn to victory only by Reynolds and Doubleday himself. In the 1870s he secured the right to author *Chancellorsville and Gettysburg* for the Scribner's war history series, and continued his diatribe as ostensibly objective history. He died in 1893, convinced that his talents and contributions had been overlooked in preference for those of lesser men. Not very many people agreed with him. Abner Doubleday, in short, was a mediocre to competent field commander with an ego to match his aspirations rather than his skills, and as such was no different from dozens of other officer, Union and Confederate.

Except for one decision, made about noon, July 1, 1863.

When John Reynolds died, Abner Doubleday became not only acting commander of the I Corps, but also the senior Federal officer at Gettysburg. Though he had no inkling that Meade would replace him with Newton, he did realize that Major General Oliver Otis Howard, commanding XI Corps, was riding toward the battlefield at the head of his own divisions, and that once Howard arrived he would take command by virtue of superior rank. Unfortunately, as the sun reached its zenith and Lieutenant Colonel Dawes began sorting out his prisoners in the railroad cut, Doubleday had no idea just *when* Howard would arrive.

Major General Abner Doubleday.
(Library of Congress)

**Abner Doubleday
monument at
Gettysburg.**

He had to assume, given the fact that there were at least two more Rebel divisions within supporting distance of Heth's somewhat battered command, that the Army of Northern Virginia would sooner or later make another push towards Gettysburg. And he had to plan as if the now-bloodied I Corps (plus Buford's thoroughly jaded cavalry) was all he had to meet it. Should he continue to defend McPherson's Ridge, pull back to Seminary Ridge (the last defensible line west of Gettysburg), or retreat south of the town toward Cemetery Hill?

Complicating matters, Doubleday had no idea precisely what had been in Reynolds's mind before he died. The last time he had seen the corps commander, the instructions he had received involved a vague injunction to superintend the southern end of the existing Federal line. Doubleday had not been privy to the messages Reynolds sent to Meade and other corps commanders, bringing on a general concentration of the army, and there were apparently no staff officers around to tell him. As Jacob Slagle, one of Doubleday's staff officers, later wrote, his commander felt a heavy weight hanging over him, "as he was not informed of Reynolds' plans." In a moment when there was no luxury for Doubleday to pace and consider for an extended period, he did something that most of his officers had trouble believing—he made a quick decision. McPherson's Ridge would be held.

Later he would explain the rationale in his usual, pedantic style: "as General Reynolds, who was high in the confidence of General Meade, had formed his lines to resist the entrance of the enemy into Gettysburg, I naturally supposed that it was the intention to defend the place." Undoubtedly, however, at least three other considerations played into Doubleday's decision. First—and perhaps even foremost—came pride, not individual *hubris*, but rock-solid unit pride. McPherson's Ridge, from the woods to the railroad cut, represented ground that I Corps had fought and bled for; soldiers like the midwesterners of the Iron Brigade or those New Yorkers and Pennsylvanians of Cutler's brigade did not consider such issues lightly—nor did their commanders. Then there was the question of whether Seminary Ridge actually provided better defensive terrain. The existence of Willoughby Run and McPherson's Woods west of McPherson's Ridge both granted a careful defender tactical advantages that could offset enemy weight of numbers; moreover, while Seminary Ridge would also be difficult for the Rebels to assault, Gettysburg lay directly behind it. If Doubleday predicated his defense on holding Seminary Ridge, he would have no ground left upon which a rear guard might hold off the Confederates while his own men retreated through the streets of the town.

Finally, Doubleday—like Buford before him—had to consider the negatives of dropping back to Cemetery Hill. Even assuming that Lee's army would not attempt to crush him during his withdrawal, and allowing for the fact that Cemetery Hill and Culp's Hill possessed even more strengths as defensive terrain, there remained a major objection to such a move. Like Buford, Doubleday realized that if he gambled on holding Cemetery Hill and lost it before sufficient reinforcements came up, he might very well be losing the entire battle before it was truly started. Fighting for McPherson's Ridge risked the outright destruction of I Corps, no two ways about it, but even that destruction could prove meaningful if it gave the rest of the army time to deploy. And if he could make the Confederates pay for every inch of ground. . . .

In the end, Doubleday opted for a strategy similar to that which Buford had employed: defense in depth. This time, however, instead of being the last line of defense McPherson's Ridge would become his outlier and he would stage his reserves off Seminary Ridge. Of Wadsworth's 1st Division, Meredith's Iron Brigade remained in McPherson's Woods near Willoughby Run. The regiments on either flank—the 2nd Wisconsin on the right and 24th Michigan on the left—had taken the heaviest casualties in the earlier fighting with Archer's Brigade, so Doubleday had them switched to the interior of the line, placing the 7th Wisconsin and 19th Indiana on the respective flanks. Dawes's 6th Wisconsin remained detached with Cutler's brigade, which—counting the morning's losses, probably left Meredith with eleven hundred officers and men at a critical point where the Confederates were sure to renew the attack. Cutler's shot-up brigade, even with the addition of the 6th Wisconsin, had only about 1,240 men available, and at least three of his regiments (the 56th Pennsylvania, 76th and 147th New York) were still reorganizing in Shead's Woods on Seminary Ridge. They had, however, finally been reunited with the 14th Brooklyn and 95th New York, so Cutler would be able to fight his whole command as a unit again. Doubleday planned to have Cutler eventually move back up to McPherson's Ridge to support some artillery just north of Chambersburg Pike.

In the meantime, Doubleday's own 3rd Division, now commanded by Brigadier General Thomas Rowley, had arrived, providing another 4,701 men to buck up the defense. Colonel Roy Stone's brigade (the 143rd, 149th, and 150th Pennsylvania) took the position on the Iron Brigade's flank between McPherson's Woods and Chambersburg Pike, which had previously been held by the two detached regiments of Cutler's brigade; Stone had 1,315 men. The most disquieting aspect of this deployment was the fact that, Cutler not yet having moved up from Seminary Ridge, Stone's right flank was hanging in the air, vulnerable to any Rebel force that might come crashing in from the north. Rowley's other brigade (Colonel Chapman Biddle with the 1,361 men of the 80th New York and the 121st, 142nd, and 151st Pennsylvania) took up a position on the reverse slope of McPherson's Ridge, staggered behind and slightly to the left of the Iron Brigade.

Brigadier General John C. Robinson ("the hairiest man in an army of bearded generals") commanded the 2nd Division, which was the last to arrive. Initially, Doubleday intended this division as his reserve, placing the 1,178 men of Brigadier General Henry Baxter's 2nd Brigade consisting of six small regiments (the 12th Massachusetts; 83rd and 97th New York; 11th, 88th, and 90th Pennsylvania) on the reverse slope of Seminary Ridge behind Cutler. At the same time, Brigadier General Gabriel Paul's 1st Brigade (the 16th Maine; 13th Massachusetts; 94th and 104th New York; 107th Pennsylvania), fell in directly west of the Lutheran Seminary, backstopping Biddle's command. With

This photo taken just a few days after the battle shows the McPherson farm as it looked in 1863. *(GNMP)*

This photo taken after the battle shows the condition of the corn-field and the grove-like appearance of McPherson's woods. The fencing between the woods and the cornfield was knocked down during the battle. *(Library of Congress)*

1,537 men present for duty, Paul had the largest I Corps brigade on the field. Doubleday's infantry deployment was an improvisation built around the existing positions of Wadsworth's two brigades, with new units plugged into gaps as they arrived on the field. As such it had two potential weaknesses, one serious and the other difficult to calculate. The most serious deficiency in this defense was that Doubleday kept all of his troops facing west, even though he knew that the next Rebel attack was just as likely to come from the north. True, he had Devin's cavalry videttes to provide an early warning, and he had dashed off a message to Howard, asking for a XI Corps division to hold his right flank. (Howard would respond by sending two divisions, six thousand men, but not before the Confederates attacked.) Even so, an enemy unit of significant strength on Oak Ridge had the potential to roll up the entire McPherson's Ridge defense. Once Doubleday realized that he would not receive XI

Present-day photo looking west from McPherson's Ridge toward Willoughby Run. Note the apparent lack of slope from this angle.

Corps reinforcements in time, he ordered Baxter's brigade moved north of Cutler to hold his right flank, extending his already thinly manned line and committing half of his reserve force before the battle opened. Still, having made the decision to defend McPherson's Ridge, it is difficult to find a better alternative.

The second potential weakness was more of an intangible. Doubleday's deployment broke up the three divisions of the I Corps into their constituent brigades. None of the corps' six brigades actually stood adjacent to a unit from its own division, which meant that most of the orders would have to come directly from corps headquarters, bypassing the division commanders. The problem was not that six brigades (about eight thousand men) was too large a command for a single officer; each of Lee's infantry divisions averaged four or five brigades and about that many men. Instead, the concern was what to do about those now essentially supernumerary division commanders roaming around the battlefield—especially James Wadsworth. Wadsworth and Doubleday never got along that well in the first place, and there is no evidence of the acting corps commander attempting to issue his orders through the division commander, or even that Doubleday explained his defensive concept to his ranking subordinate. Wadsworth seems to have contented himself with riding around McPherson's Ridge passing out his own orders, without the slightest notion of how they might interfere with Doubleday's own instructions (and completely without regard for such niceties as which units were actually under his nominal command). Within an hour, for example, Wadsworth had authorized Cutler's brigade to withdraw toward Cemetery Hill (countermanded by Doubleday); deployed a field battery into a dangerously exposed position (countermanded by Wainwright); and ordered Stone's Brigade to send out three companies of skirmishers across Willoughby Run (countermanded by no one, since no one else appears to have discovered it). It was impossible to predict how much of a factor Wadsworth's freelance leadership might become when the Rebels attacked again.

Finally, it should be noted that Doubleday's artillery deployment was somewhat haphazard, despite the best that Charles Wainwright could do to correct it. Calef's Battery B, 4th U. S. Artillery, had unlimbered on the left flank of Cutler's brigade, aiming west toward Herr Ridge. Near Paul's brigade and the Lutheran Seminary stood the 5th Maine Battery, also training six guns to the west. Battery L, 1st New York, dropped trails at the right flank of Biddle's brigade, facing north, while Battery B, 1st Pennsylvania, was behind Biddle's brigade (in the swale between McPherson's and Seminary Ridges) also firing north. Thus, of the twenty-one guns immediately available to Wainwright (Hall's 2nd Maine was still reorganizing), eleven faced west and ten toward the north, with the individual batteries so spaced across the field that it would be difficult to concentrate fire on a single target.

None of these deployments, infantry or artillery, took place in a parade-ground atmosphere. Heth's infantry may have momentarily let up the pressure as he changed the brigades on the line of assault, but Pegram's artillery kept up a continuous fire on those Union positions he could see from Herr Ridge. In particular, Battery l, 1st New York, and Biddle's brigade came in for the attention of Confederate artillerymen. Lying flat on the ground behind McPherson's Ridge, Biddle's relatively green brigade (only the 80th New York could truly be considered a veteran outfit) took a demoralizing pounding from gunners the soldiers could not even see. Perhaps the stress of having to passively accept that shelling explained the reaction of Private John Weber, Company F, 150th Pennsylvania of Stone's Brigade—also a favorite target of Rebel gunners—who leapt maniacally to his feet, shouting, "Come, boys, choose your partners! The ball is about to open! Don't you hear the music?"

On the Confederate side of the line, strange as it still

seems, no corps commander had yet arrived to take control of the battle. A. P. Hill, having remained in his Cashtown headquarters during the morning's fight (suffering from symptoms of his gonorrhea and the psychological stress of being a corps commander), had finally been prompted some time after noon by General Lee himself to ride out and discover what all the gunfire toward Gettysburg was about. Lee had cautioned all of his subordinates that he did not want "a general engagement" started until the entire army was up, and Lieutenant General James Longstreet's I Corps remained miles to the west. On the other hand, the Confederate army commander badly needed to know precisely *where* the main body of the Army of the Potomac was to be located. Major General J. E. B. Stuart was absent on a raid with the most reliable cavalry units in the army (still the subject of major controversy today), leaving Lee groping around central Pennsylvania like a blind man, trying to find his opponent.

Thus the 24,000 Rebels within reach of Gettysburg by noon on July 1 fought under three brand-new division commanders from two different corps, while the bulk of the III Corps artillery appeared to take part in the fighting almost as independent contractors. Along Herr Ridge, Henry Heth was busily re-forming his division for another attack, while Pender's Division deployed into line of battle to his rear. Coming in from the north was the army's largest division, 7,983 men and sixteen guns under Major General Robert Rodes of Ewell's II Corps. No one exercised overall command, no one even appears to have coordinated operations between the two corps. Rodes's attack in the Oak Ridge sector would come as almost as big a surprise to Heth as it did to Doubleday. Pender deferred to Heth in a most peculiar manner, allowing the Virginian to keep on fighting his own private battle without every raising the issue of whether or not his division might be better employed in swinging around Doubleday's left flank for a quick knock-out.

Heth left Davis's bloodied brigade on his left flank, giving up any idea of striking the Federals north of Chambersburg Pike. Not in quite as bad a condition, though its numbers had been reduced to about one thousand, Archer's Brigade (now commanded by Colonel Fry) slid south down Herr Ridge to constitute the division's right wing. Immediately south of the pike, facing Stone's Pennsylvanians, Heth placed Brockenbrough's 40th, 47th, and 55th Virginia and the 22nd Virginia Battalion, while James Pettigrew's much larger brigade (composed of the 11th, 26th, 47th, and 52nd North Carolina) extended down the ridge far beyond the Iron Brigade's open southern flank. Between Brockenbrough and Pettigrew, Heth could throw about 3,555 men against the 2,400 possessed by Stone and Meredith. Such was the confusion on Herr Ridge in the aftermath of Archer's rebuff and Davis's thrashing, however, that these two brigades would not be ready to attack until 2:30 P.M.

In the interim, the two leading brigades of Rodes's Division, under Brigadier Generals Alfred Iverson and Junius Daniel, would make their own bloody, disjointed entrance into the fight.

CHAPTER 7

SPRAYED BY THE BRAINS OF THE FIRST RANK

ALFRED IVERSON WAS A GEORGIAN commanding a brigade of North Carolinians, which was a large part of the problem. State attachments being at the very foundation of Confederate identity, Lee made consistent efforts to keep as many regiments as possible brigaded together by states and commanded by natives as well. A strange concatenation of events, however, had catapulted Iverson into his Tarheel command, and an even more unfortunate set of circumstances set him so hopelessly at odds with his own officers and men that they entered the Gettysburg campaign in a state of near-mutiny, willing to believe the worst of their commander.

The thirty-four-year-old son of a Georgia politician, Iverson had as much military background as many Confederate brigadiers; before becoming an attorney and railroad contractor, he had graduated from the Tuskegee Military Institute and served as a lieutenant in the Mounted Rifles during the Mexican War. Then, in 1855, he was one of several men selected from civilian life for a commission in one of the U. S. Army's newest regiments, becoming a lieutenant in the 1st U. S. Cavalry, a position he held through the Mormon Expedition and forays against the Kiowas and Comanches, until secession caused him to resign and return home. Appointed into the Provisional Army of the Confederate States and initially assigned to duty in Wilmington, North Carolina, Iverson assisted in the recruiting and organization of several companies of the 20th North Carolina, and shortly thereafter was elected the regiment's colonel. He won the approbation of his superiors in that position at Gaines' Mill in the Seven Days Battles, and succeeded Samuel Garland to brigade command after that officer fell in the Antietam campaign. Prewar photographs of Iverson reveal a slender, serious figure, who gazed intently at the camera while seeming somehow uncomfortable with the lens and flash that invaded his privacy. A reserved, private man who wrote poetry and read Shakespeare for recreation, Iverson lacked the popular touch of a John Bell Hood or Robert Rodes. Despite his excellent horsemanship and military bearing, his men remembered him more as a stern disciplinarian. Yet Iverson enjoyed a reasonably good rapport with his officers—at least for the first month.

In December 1862, the colonelcy of his old regiment having been vacated by his promotion, Iverson stunned his entire brigade by recommending—instead of his own field officers—Lieutenant Colonel William S. DeVane of the 61st North Carolina, an old friend then serving on the South Carolina coast. This attempt to bring in an outsider enraged his officers, twenty-six of whom signed a protest to Adjutant and Inspector General Samuel Cooper. Iverson read the document and refused to forward it; when they did so without his signature, he ordered the arrest of every man who had signed it. Although Iverson backed down a few weeks later, the damage had been done. As Lieutenant O. E. Mercer of Company G, 20th North Carolina, wrote, "Iverson is very unpopular with the Brigade. . . ."

Not surprisingly, when Iverson absented himself at a critical moment at Chancellorsville to seek reinforcements (which he found) and did not return before the fighting ended (having been wounded painfully though not seriously, in the groin), there were whispers of cowardice. When his division liberated a considerable store of whiskey at Carlisle, Pennsylvania, on June 29, Iverson (who had spent several years there with his now-deceased wife) imbibed a little too freely. General Rodes and several other officers got more than a little inebriated that afternoon as well, but only Iverson suffered from the quickly circulating rumor that he was a drunkard as well as a poltroon.

Then fate placed Iverson and the 1,384 men of the 5th, 12th, 20th, and 23rd North Carolina at the head of Rodes's Division marching into Gettysburg on July 1. The tactical situation confronting Rodes (in his first battle as a full-fledged major general) was admittedly difficult. He swept Devin's cavalry off of Oak Hill with little difficulty just before noon and contemplated his next move. Southeast of Oak Hill lay Oak Ridge (which was really the northern extension of Seminary Ridge), where Cutler's battered brigade lay on Doubleday's open flank. A bit further to the east Rodes's field glasses could discern the lead elements of Howard's XI Corps moving through Gettysburg, obviously intent on extending and protecting Doubleday's line. If he moved quickly enough, Rodes realized that he could "strike the force of the enemy with which General Hill's troops were engaged upon the flank, and that, besides moving under cover, whenever we struck the enemy we could engage him with the advantage in ground." The catch was that he would have to commit his division to attacking the center of a two-corps line before Major General Jubal Early's Division arrived, and without any time to communicate with whoever was controlling the III Corps units west of McPherson's Ridge. Nor would there be the luxury of probing the enemy position to be completely sure of the Federal dispositions. To score a decisive victory, Rodes would have to strike fast; *too* fast, as events would prove.

Rodes left Brigadier General George Doles's Brigade on his left flank to observe the arrival of the XI Corps, and held Brigadier General Stephen Ramseur's regiments in

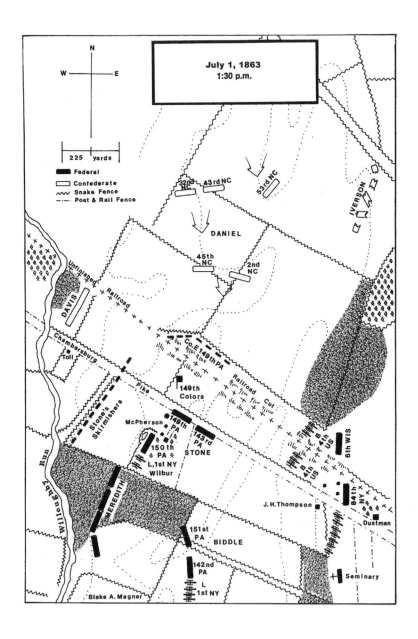

division reserve, while concentrating all sixteen guns of his division artillery on Oak Hill to support a three-brigade drive down Oak Ridge by Iverson, Brigadier General Junius Daniel, and Colonel Edward A. O'Neal. Between them these brigades numbered 5,234 men. O'Neal received the most difficult assignment, at least in terms of troop management. Rodes directed him to leave his 5th Alabama behind to connect with Doles's Brigade, and then sweep down Oak Ridge by straddling the height with the 6th, 12th, and 26th Alabama on the eastern slope and the 3rd Alabama on the western side of the ridge to maintain contact with Iverson's Brigade. That O'Neal never actually understood his instructions is made clear in reading his official report; accompanying the three eastern regiments he did not even realize the roles intended for the 3rd and 5th Alabama: "Why my brigade was thus deprived of two regiments, I have never been informed." Iverson, though "not understanding the exact time at which the advance was to take place," knew that he was supposed to move forward when he saw O'Neal start out (though he could only see the 3rd Alabama) and notify Daniel to follow on his right flank. This was also Daniel's understanding of the mission.

Unfortunately, Colonel Cullen A. Battle of the 3rd Alabama, whose regiment held the key position connecting Iverson and O'Neal, had a completely different idea about what he was supposed to be doing. Battle, an outstanding tactician in his own right, understood that he was supposed to align his advance not on Iverson's Brigade, but on Daniel's; he apparently did not even know about Iverson's role in the attack "until Daniel moved to the support of Iverson. . . ." Then, because he shared O'Neal's misperception that he had been completely detached from his own brigade, Battle "sent an officer to General Daniel for orders, who on his return reported to me that General Daniel said he had no orders for me, and that I must act on my own responsibility." Thus the fruits of Rodes's haste to launch his attack were that none of his three senior subordinates completely understood the division commander's intent. The colonel commanding the regiment in the critical position between Iverson and O'Neal did not even know who was supposed to give him his orders; and Oak Ridge kept the bulk of one brigade totally out of sight from the other two. As a recipe for disaster, it contained all the necessary ingredients.

To make matters worse, O'Neal's three regiments ran into Federal skirmishers as they approached Mummasburg Road, which crossed the northern end of Oak Ridge. Confused about his orders and taking enemy fire, Colonel O'Neal never managed to advance, and failed to alert anyone else to his situation. On the other side of Oak Ridge, however, Colonel Battle did move his 3rd Alabama forward as he saw Iverson come onto the field, which in turn led Iverson to believe that O'Neal's other regiments had begun the attack east of Oak Ridge. Because he thought everything was proceeding according to plan, Iverson left his troops momentarily to confer with Daniels. His four colonels, thinking that they were still hundreds of yards away from first contact with the enemy and secure on both flanks, marched their men south in column formation at shoulder arms, rifles not yet loaded. These miscues might have proven difficult rather than disastrous, except for the man in command of the Union brigade that had been rushed up to cover Cutler's flank—Brigadier General Henry Baxter.

By July 1, 1863, the men under Baxter's command must have wondered precisely what it would take to kill him. Forty-two years old, Baxter had been born in New York and immigrated to Michigan, where, except for a two-year excursion into the California gold fields from 1849–1851, he worked as a miller, until accepting a commission as a captain in the 7th Michigan in 1861. During the Seven Days, Baxter took a round to the stomach; after dodging peritonitis, he received promotion to lieutenant colonel. At

Antietam, he was shot in the lung, a wound from which he miraculously managed to recover in time to participate in the battle of Fredericksburg, two months later. There Baxter led a forlorn hope of seventy men across the Rappahannock River to drive away the Rebel sharpshooters who were keeping the Army of the Potomac's engineers from completing their pontoon bridges. He accomplished his mission at the cost of a minie ball shattering his shoulder; recuperating, he abruptly found himself wearing the star of a brigadier general.

When Devin's retreat from Oak Hill forewarned Doubleday that the Rebels were advancing from the north before the XI Corps could get into position, he ordered Baxter's 2nd Brigade out of its reserve position to form at right angles to Cutler's command. Paul's brigade, further to the south, would follow, shifting all of Robinson's 2nd Division to the I Corps right flank. Baxter immediately deployed the 11th Pennsylvania and 97th New York (506 men) on Cutler's immediate right, then moved forward toward the Mummasburg Road with the remaining 946 men of the 12th Massachusetts, 83rd New York, and 88th and 90th Pennsylvania, throwing out several companies of skirmishers north of that road. Since Baxter's four regiments moved along the eastern slope of Oak Ridge, neither Battle nor Iverson saw the maneuver.

When Baxter's skirmishers halted O'Neal's three regiments in their tracks, the Yankee commander (who had sent scouts to the top of the ridge) realized that two more Rebel brigades were attacking south, just out of his line of vision. Without hesitation, Baxter left only a few companies of the 12th Massachusetts to delay O'Neal and marched the rest of his command by the left flank over Oak Ridge, managing to position them behind a stone fence without being detected by either Battle or Iverson. Iverson's Tarheels—still marching in column with unloaded weapons—had meanwhile drifted in their commander's absence into almost a left wheel, leaving them nearly parallel to Oak

Ridge and only eighty yards away from nearly one thousand Yankees whose presence they did not suspect.

What happened when Baxter's four regiments opened fire on Iverson's compact, parade ground ranks is most accurately described as slaughter. One 23rd North Carolina private in the second rank "was sprayed by the brains of the first rank," as hundreds of Confederates fell to the first volley, many dying in straight lines as they had marched. The survivors "went to ground," dropping into small folds in the earth, trying desperately to find cover, but within minutes Paul's brigade had come up on Baxter's left, more than doubling the number of Federals firing into Iverson's shattered regiments. This situation held for the next thirty to forty-five minutes, as the deadly fire found almost any Carolinian brave or foolish enough to raise his head; as Lieutenant Oliver Williams of the 20th North Carolina recalled, "Every man who stood up was either killed or wounded." One body of a soldier from the 5th North Carolina would later be found riddled with bullets, including no fewer than five holes in his skull. Colonel Daniel H. Christie of the 23rd North Carolina took a mortal wound trying gamely to organize a rush at the stone wall, along with dozens more who followed him.

At length, assured that O'Neal was not about to advance east of the ridge to threaten their rear, Baxter and Paul delivered the *coup de grace*, charging across the short distance separating them from their victims, capturing hundreds of (mostly wounded) prisoners, and seizing three regimental flags. In less than one hour, the two Federal brigades had fired over one hundred thousand rounds at near pointblank range into fewer than fourteen hundred Rebels. Iverson's brigade lost 455 killed and wounded, along with about 500 prisoners, virtually gutting every regiment except the 12th North Carolina, of which eight companies had been spared the worst of the killing by having fallen behind and out of alignment. The regiments directly involved in the debacle suffered 71 percent casualties, worse even than those inflicted on the brigades that attacked Cemetery Ridge two days later.

Baxter (with an assist from Paul) had achieved the near-annihilation of a force 25 percent larger than his own. Better yet, for the first time in a major battle, Baxter himself escaped unwounded. When O'Neal, now supported by Ramseur, finally attacked east of Oak Ridge, Baxter and Paul shifted part of their troops to meet this belated threat, giving ground grudgingly over successive lines of resistance as the XI Corps fell in on their right flank. Any chance that Rodes had to crack open the Federal line with one decisive strike had evaporated before 1:00 P.M.

The final casualty was Alfred Iverson himself. His absence from his command, though justifiable in hindsight at the range of more than a century, confirmed nearly everyone's suspicions of cowardice. Rodes (who certainly shared in the responsibility for his brigade's destruction) refused to speak with him, and dying in his hospital bed Colonel Christie told everyone that while "he might never live to lead them in battle . . . he would see that 'the imbecile Iverson' never should either." The remnants of Iverson's regiments were attached to Ramseur's Brigade, and upon the army's return to Pennsylvania, Lee had the young Georgian transferred out of the Army of Northern Virginia as tactfully as possible.

(Iverson, who fell into serious depression over the incident, eventually recovered. His father's political clout sufficed to secure him a position commanding a brigade of Georgia State Guards in late 1863, and when their six-month enlistments expired in February 1864, Iverson ended up in command of a Georgia cavalry brigade in the Army of Tennessee during the Atlanta campaign. Not only did he serve competently there as a brigade and division commander for the rest of the war, almost two years after Gettysburg he achieved some measure of personal revenge for his earlier defeat. At the battle of Sunshine Church, south of Atlanta, Iverson's cavalry gutted a raiding Union division, and captured George Stoneman, the only Federal major general taken prisoner on the battlefield.)

Baxter's victory, Doubleday soon realized, had not ended the threat from Rodes's Division. On Iverson's right there remained Daniel's heretofore-unengaged brigade of nearly twenty-two hundred more North Carolinians. Perplexed by the initial "change of direction" when Iverson's regiments had begun drifting toward Oak Ridge, and "having received no notification" about such a modification, Daniel was totally unprepared for Baxter's attack. With the actual situation obscured by billowing clouds of smoke, Daniel understood only that "General Iverson became engaged with the enemy." With the stentorian speaking voice that usually marked his commands, Daniel bellowed orders for three of his own regiments (the 32nd, 43rd, and 53rd North Carolina) to swing around toward the left, intending to keep himself on Iverson's right flank as originally planned. His remaining two units, the 45th North Carolina and 2nd North Carolina Battalion (810 strong), continued south toward Chambersburg Pike, only to run afoul—as Joseph Davis had two hours earlier—of that damnable railroad cut.

CHAPTER 8

A FURIOUS MUSKETRY FIRE

THERE WAS NOTHING ABOUT HIS POSITION that Colonel Roy Stone liked. His three regiments of Pennsylvania Bucktails had been assigned the same line held in the morning by Fowler's detachment of Cutler's brigade: the western slope of McPherson's Ridge, north of McPherson's Woods and south of Chambersburg Pike. According to Doubleday's original defensive scheme, once Cutler's brigade had reorganized in Shead's Woods on Seminary Ridge, it was to move forward north of the road and cover Stone's right flank. Other than a single, tentative movement, easily discouraged by Rebel artillery, however, Cutler had remained in the safety of the woods, leaving Stone's Pennsylvanians on the far end of an advanced and very exposed line. The best that Stone could do, with Heth's Division staring down at him from Herr Ridge, was to risk placing the 450 men of Lieutenant Colonel Walton Dwight's 149th Pennsylvania at a right angle to his main line, parallel to Chambersburg Pike, facing north. A single regiment might not be able to do much about a major Confederate attack, but at least Dwight could let him know it was coming.

This deployment left Stone with only the 865 troops of Colonel Edmund Dana's 143rd Pennsylvania and Colonel Langhorne Wister's 150th Pennsylvania to face whatever Heth might throw across Willoughby Run. The men were tired if not quite exhausted, their faces caked with gray dust from the march to Gettysburg, which had grown increasingly fast-paced as the battle heated up and staff officers had been sent to hurry them along. At some point in the early afternoon, General Wadsworth rode up, and though he was neither Stone's division commander nor entrusted with any special mission by Doubleday, ordered a company of skirmishers from each regiment sent as far forward as possible. Stone plainly thought that this was a waste; he could clearly see any move the Confederates made to come down off Herr Ridge, and the subtraction of three companies left him with fewer than seven hundred muskets in his main battle line as the continuing Rebel artillery harassment took a small, continuous toll on his numbers as well. His skirmishers, however, had "to advance over an open field, without the slightest shelter, and under a hot fire from the enemy's skirmishers concealed behind a fence. . . ."

Colonel Roy Stone.
(USAMHI)

Some time before 1:00 P.M., Rodes's artillery appeared on Oak Hill, far off on Stone's right, and began the fire that sent Cutler back to the trees and forced the 149th Pennsylvania to change its position. "About 1:30 P.M. the grand advance of the enemy began," Stone later reported, meaning that Iverson and Daniel had come out of concealment and begun the two-mile approach march toward the Chambersburg Pike. Dwight's men could see them clearly, "a nearly continuous line of deployed battalions, with other battalions in mass or reserve." Stone also noted when Iverson's Brigade started drifting east, "thus causing a break in their line and exposing the flank of those engaged" with Baxter's men behind the stone wall. More as a defiant gesture than anything else (the range was extreme) Stone allowed the regiment to open fire on Iverson's 12th North Carolina.

Seeing nothing happening across on Herr Ridge, Stone had risked moving Dana's 143rd Pennsylvania into line with the 149th on Chambersburg Pike, effectively reversing the intent of Doubleday's original deployment by facing two-thirds of his command to the north rather than the east. As it turned out, this was the right decision, made in a timely manner. Only a few minutes after the second regiment had maneuvered into position, Stone realized that his enemies had organized "a heavy force . . . formed in two lines parallel to the Chambersburg road," which "pressed forward to the attack of my position." These lines belonged to the 45th North Carolina and 2nd North Carolina Battalion of Daniel's Brigade.

Five days past his thirty-fifth birthday, Junius Daniel was one of the up-and-coming professional brigade commanders (West Point, 1851) out of North Carolina who formed part of the backbone of Lee's army. Known for his frontline leadership (one horse was shot from under him at Malvern Hill) and a stentorian voice that could be heard, it seemed, for nearly a mile across a noisy battlefield, Daniel and his Tarheels liked nothing better than to be sent straight at the

General Junius Daniel.
(Library of Congress)

enemy's critical point. Unfortunately, this day Daniel was about as frustrated and confused as Colonel Stone. When Iverson's Brigade began its fatal wheel to the left, Daniel initially thought that Rodes had ordered some change in the attack plan, and "having received no notification of his change of direction, I allowed my line to move on, and rode to the front to reconnoiter." He discovered Baxter's terrible ambush of Iverson's regiments, and quickly attempted to cover the other brigade's exposed right flank with most of his own command, leaving just two units moving toward Stone's position along the Chambersburg Pike.

It was the kind of opportunistic decision expected of a brigade commander in the Army of Northern Virginia. Daniel realized that, if he did nothing but support Iverson's men, Rodes's entire attack would end in a bloody repulse that gained no ground and did the Yankees no harm. On the other hand, he had seen Cutler's brigade pull back to Seminary Ridge, leaving the entire Union position along the western slope of McPherson's Ridge vulnerable to a flank attack. Daniel did not know for certain when Heth would advance, but the North Carolinian realized that with a little luck even his small thrust could be the force that unbalanced the Federal line. For this gamble he had his own former regiment, the 45th North Carolina under Lieutenant Colonel Samuel H. Boyd, and Lieutenant Colonel Hezekiah S. Andrews's 2nd North Carolina Battalion (a unit short on discipline but long on fight—Daniel often referred to it as "my little mob").

With nearly equal numbers (810 Carolinians attacking about 800 Pennsylvanians), Daniels's men would appear to have been at a disadvantage, but it must be remembered that Stone's Bucktails were both exhausted and had been subjected to strong Confederate artillery fire from two directions for at least an hour. Moreover, it was at this inopportune moment that skirmish firing along Willoughby Run began to increase, suggesting that Heth's attack could not be far off. Given the disjointed nature of the fighting that had already occurred, it was hardly unthinkable that Daniel's men might just succeed.

Except for the railroad cut. . . .

Present-day photo looking southwest from the northern end of McPherson's Ridge at the railroad cut. Note that all you can see is a wandering line of trees and not the cut itself.

The Tarheels expected to weather at least one, if not two volleys from the Bucktails before they closed the range, and the disciplined fire from the 143rd and 149th Pennsylvania's Enfields indeed staggered their line for a time, but the Rebels came on. Only for another few moments, however, because—as Daniel admitted—"at the railroad cut, which had been partially concealed by the long grass growing around it, and which, in consequence of the abruptness of its sides, was impassable, the advance was stopped." Captain J. A. Hopkins of the 45th North Carolina was less circumspect: "about a fourth of the regiment went to the bottom. The rest fell back some 50 paces." Major John D. Musser of the 143rd Pennsylvania recorded that the Carolinians withdrew "in less numbers, and in considerable confusion."

Colonel Stone realized that the several hundred Rebels remaining in the railroad cut represented a continuing danger to his position. At any moment Daniel might reinforce them with as many as another one thousand men, creating an attacking avalanche he would not be able to hold back. Thus he decided almost instantly that, despite the risk, the railroad cut had to be cleared of the enemy. He ordered Lieutenant Colonel Dwight's 149th Pennsylvania to charge the Confederates before they could regroup. In ordering this attack, Stone also conducted one of the most imaginative tactical maneuvers of the battle. Realizing that Rebel artillery had the capability to tear Dwight's men apart, he sent the regiment's color guard twenty yards beyond the end of the 149th's line. There the small knot of soldiers stood and died, proudly waving the regimental flag and taking the brunt of the enemy artillery fire.

Over the next hour, wrote Colonel Wister, "a furious musketry fire was again going on along the whole line," as the contest between Daniel's North Carolinians and Stone's Pennsylvanians descended into the sort of brutal slugging match that is difficult to reconstruct from the conflicting reports filed by the surviving officers. Dwight's men drove the enemy from the railroad cut, and Stone apparently intended to order them back toward Chambersburg Pike. Before he could deliver this command, however, Stone was wounded and command fell to Colonel Langhorne Wister, whose 150th Pennsylvania was still facing west. Dwight, convinced that he had scored a major victory, kept his regiment in the railroad cut. Daniel reinforced his next attack with Colonel Edmund C. Brabble's 32nd North Carolina, which Captain Van Brown reported as "protracted and bloody." Dwight lost the railroad cut and at least 250–275 men, but now supported by Lieutenant James Steward's Battery B, 4th U. S. Artillery, the Federals grimly refused to be pushed back beyond their original position. By 2:30 P.M. the two brigades had fought each other out. Stone's Pennsylvanians (now commanded by Colonel Dana) had held their ground, but Daniel's North Carolinians had only retired about two hundred yards to the north to a position on the *eastern* slope of McPherson's Ridge. There they waited for Heth's attack.

Colonel Langhorne Wister. *(USAMHI)*

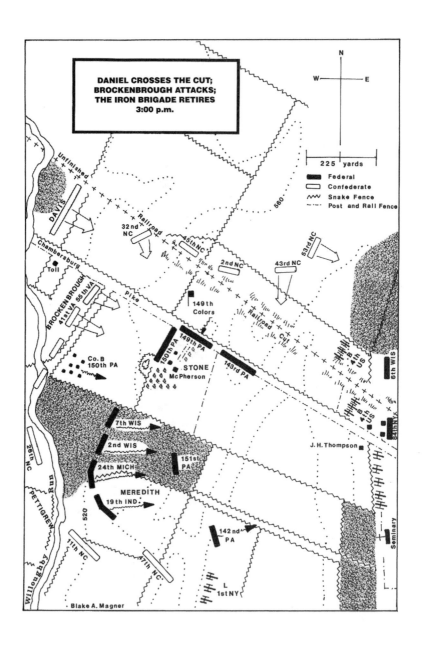

DANIEL CROSSES THE CUT;
BROCKENBROUGH ATTACKS;
THE IRON BRIGADE RETIRES
3:00 p.m.

225 yards

Federal
Confederate
Snake Fence
Post and Rail Fence

Unfinished
DAVIS
Railroad
32nd NC
45th NC
2nd NC
43rd NC
53rd NC

Chambersburg
Toll
Pike
BROCKENBROUGH
41st VA
55th VA
149th Colors
149th PA
150th PA
143rd PA
Railroad Cut
2nd US
2nd US
6th WIS

Co. B
150th PA
STONE
McPherson
7th WIS
2nd WIS
24th MICH
151st PA
19th IND
MEREDITH
J.H. Thompson
24th NY

26th NC
520
142nd PA
Seminary

11th NC
47th NC
1st NY
L

PETTIGREW
Willoughby Run

Blake A. Magner

CHAPTER 9

NOT A SHADOW OF A CHANCE

IN THE END, TWO FACTORS SETTLED THE FIGHT for McPherson's Ridge. To the north, by 2:30 P.M. Doubleday could already hear the firing between Howard's XI Corps and Major General Jubal Early's Division, which had marched up to reinforce Rodes. If the XI Corps crumpled (as it eventually would), then McPherson's Ridge would become strategically untenable, as the Rebels would then own a clear route into the I Corps's rear. The second unalterable reality that afternoon was the weight of numbers. Perhaps 300 troops from the 150th Pennsylvania still held the Iron Brigade's right flank along Willoughby Run; Meredith had roughly 1,100 men in McPherson's Woods, and the three available regiments of Colonel Biddle's brigade indirectly covering Meredith's left had only another 886 men. All told, Doubleday had barely 2,200 soldiers, directly supported by three batteries, to oppose 3,200–3,500 Rebels and at least three artillery battalions. To make matters worse, both the Iron Brigade and the 150th Pennsylvania could only be described as exhausted; Heth's attacking brigades were both unbloodied to this point in the battle.

The problem was not so much that the weight of the Confederate regiments could overwhelm the Yankees by direct assault, but that Heth could outflank any line Doubleday might place. Brockenbrough's small Virginia brigade covered the front of the 150th Pennsylvania, as well as the 2nd and 7th Wisconsin. This allowed Heth to

On the Pennsylvania memorial at Gettysburg this engraving depicts the men of the 150th Pennsylvania confronting Brockenbrough and his men.

An engraving from *History of the One Hundred Fiftieth Regiment Pennsylvania Volunteers* by Thomas Chamberlin of the battle at McPherson's farm.

concentrate the 1,550 men of the 11th and 26th North Carolina against the 500 remaining in the 24th Michigan and 19th Indiana. Likewise, Pettigrew's 47th and 52nd North Carolina overlapped Biddle's 886-man line with nearly 1,200 troops. "Their line extended the front of two regiments beyond our left flank," wrote one of Biddle's regimental commanders, Colonel Theodore Gates of the 80th New York. Colonel Charles Wainwright, the corps artillery chief, who could watch the whole spectacle unfold from his position on Seminary Ridge, waxed almost philosophical about Rebels who "marched along quietly and with confidence. . . ." His field glasses sweeping the extent of the enemy lines, Wainwright wrote that "I watched them from the battery, and . . . they outflanked us at least half a mile on our left. . . ." Resigned to the inevitable, the artilleryman concluded, "There was not a shadow of a chance of our holding this ridge," and began giving orders to save his guns.

The end came rapidly. "Our ranks were broken and became massed together," reported Lieutenant Alexander Biddle of the 121st Pennsylvania, after "a crushing fire" from the 52nd North Carolina enfiladed his regiment. "The officers made every possible effort to form their men," but too many leaders fell too quickly, and "the regiment was broken and scattered. . . ." Biddle's other regiments fared little better. Colonel Gates insisted that the 80th New York "held the position until the artillery was removed, and then fell back slowly," while the brigade commander insisted that his men had stood "until, being without any support they were compelled to retire about 4:00 P.M.," and did so while fighting a tenacious rear-guard action. Colonel Biddle overstated the length of the fight by nearly an hour, and the casualty count belied any assertion that his brigade was in condition to do "good service" later that afternoon. By 4:00 P.M., including the 151st Pennsylvania (which had returned from its detached service), Biddle could find only about 390 men. He had lost 440 killed and wounded, plus another 457 missing. (In Biddle's defense, however, it must be noted that men separated from their commands in the chaos of the retreat made every effort to find their organizations. The 121st Pennsylvania brought only two officers and forty-eight men away from McPherson's Ridge, but by morning mustered seven officers and 256 men; the same could be said of other regiments.)

The Iron Brigade also died as a coherent brigade. Colonel Henry Morrow of the 24th Michigan admitted that the soldiers of the 26th North Carolina "came on with rapid strides, yelling like demons." He ordered his men to hold their fire for one crushing volley, "but the nature of the ground was such that I am inclined to think that we inflicted but little injury. . . ." Colonel William Robinson of the 7th Wisconsin managed to hold his ground against the Virginians, but knew that the brigade's left flank was being "cut up by superior numbers. . . ." He kept waiting for orders to withdraw, wondering when Meredith, or Wadsworth, or Doubleday, or *someone* would realize that to stay in McPherson's Woods was little more than tactical suicide. The orders did not come. (At least this time no one could blame General Meredith. Riding the lines to encourage his men, "Long Sol" fell severely wounded—under his horse—winning once again the respect for courage that his men could not accord his tactical acumen.)

The cost was terrible. Lieutenant Colonel William Dudley guessed that the Iron Brigade lost half the men it had deployed in McPherson's Woods. More precisely, Dudley reported that his 19th Indiana had taken 27 officers and 261 muskets into the initial fight for McPherson's Ridge, "and on rallying at Cemetery Hill, gathering in stragglers and slightly wounded, [the regiment] mustered on the morning of July 2 a squad of 9 officers and 60 men." Unfortunately, Dudley was not among them; struck in the leg, he collapsed in the last minutes of the fight and was captured. (Interestingly enough, he would be recovered two days later when the Rebels retreated from Gettysburg.) The 24th

Top: A present-day photo of McPherson's Woods, probably not as thick as it used to be.

Inset: Men of the Iron Brigade who fell in the battle on July 1. The Iron Brigade lost more than half its men in McPherson's Woods that day.

Michigan lost 316 of 496 men, the 2nd Wisconsin 233 of 302, and the 7th Wisconsin 178 of 364. In total, the four regiments of the Iron Brigade engaged on McPherson's Ridge left behind 937 of 1,450 men (65 percent). In addition, Dawes's detached 6th Wisconsin had lost another 164 casualties.

For Heth's Division success had been dearly bought. Colonel Henry King Burgwyn's 26th North Carolina started down Herr Ridge with 843 officers and men. Sergeant J. T. C. Hood of Company F recalled that the Iron Brigade's first volley "mowed us down like wheat before the sickle." The Carolinians heard the midwestern officers shouting, "Fire low! Fire low!" and Corporal James Dorsett remembered that "bullets were flying around me like hailstones in a storm. . . ." Years later Dorsett would vividly recall the gory spectacle: "Lots of men near me were falling to the ground, throwing up their arms and clawing the earth. The whole field was covered with grey suits soaked in blood." General Pettigrew, watching Burgwyn's regiment walk unswervingly into the fire and then close with the Iron Brigade in a brutal melee, sent a courier to the commander of the 26th North Carolina with the message, "Tell him his regiment has covered itself with glory today." It had also been covered in blood: when the Federals finally withdrew, Burgwyn's regiment had been reduced to 212 men.

Colonel Collett Leventhorpe's 11th North Carolina, which also faced the Iron Brigade, took 250 casualties out of 617 engaged, while the combined losses of the 47th and 52nd North Carolina against Biddle's brigade amounted to another 300 troops. Thus Pettigrew's Brigade sustained 1,100 casualties from a starting strength of 2,584 (43 percent). Brockenbrough's small command did not escape unscathed either. According to Colonel Robert M. Mayo of the 47th Virginia they suffered about 770 casualties (79 percent). In sum, Heth's two brigades had finally cleared McPherson's Ridge, but the effort effectively cost Lee's army another large brigade, not to mention more than two dozen experienced field officers. Taking the morning losses of Archer's and Davis's Brigades into account, fully half of Heth's Division had been rendered *hors de combat* in the struggle for the ridge, to which must be added the destruction of Iverson's Brigade and heavy casualties among Daniel's North Carolinians.

On the other side of the ledger, small knots of Yankees retreated across Seminary Ridge and through the streets of Gettysburg, here and there stopping to fight for a few minutes along nameless fences or behind shot-riddled buildings, bearing mute testimony to the shattering losses taken by the Army of the Potomac's I Corps. "To show the severity of the battle," Doubleday subsequently reported, "it is sufficient to state that there was hardly a field officer left unhurt. . . . The First Corps went in about 8,250 strong and came out with about 2,450." Nine months later, having failed to recruit those decimated regiments back up to strength, General Meade would reluctantly order the I Corps "temporarily" dissolved. Gettysburg on July 1 had seen the outfit's finest, but essentially final hour.

At 4 P.M. on July 1 Union artillery cover the retreat as Early's men attack the Federal lines. The battle for McPherson's Ridge was over, the battle of Gettysburg raged for two more days.

But what had been lost or won in the eight-hour battle for McPherson's Ridge? For the Confederates it is clear, first of all, that a major reason for the early difficulties in seizing the ground west of Gettysburg was the absence of cavalry. Any one of Major General J. E. B. Stuart's brigades would have been able to push Gamble's horsemen off Herr Ridge much faster than Heth's infantry, and would have left the foot soldiers unscathed for the attack on McPherson's Ridge. Moreover, cavalry would have revealed to Heth that the I Corps's left flank below the Fairfield Road remained dangerously exposed throughout the day. Had the Confederate division commander realized that he could swing one of his brigades around the end of the Federal line, he might well have broken the enemy defense much more quickly and at a much lower cost.

Yet even had Henry Heth known about that particular Yankee vulnerability he might not have exploited it. Heth's first performance as a division commander was marked by failures to see anything other than what he wanted to see and unimaginative frontal assaults. That Pettigrew divided his large brigade to out-flank Meredith and Biddle simultaneously was a credit to the North Carolinian, not his commander. Likewise, in his costly, disjointed attack down Oak Ridge, Robert Rodes proved that success as a brigadier did not necessarily translate immediately into competence at the division level. Rodes—unlike Heth—would later develop into an outstanding divisional tactician, but on his first day in command he was equally clumsy. (A large part of the indictment against Heth and Rodes, however, should be counted against Lee, Ewell, and A. P. Hill, none of whom reached the field in time to have any influence on the struggle that decided the fate of McPherson's Ridge. Allowing the opening phases of the battle to be conducted by two of the army's newest division commanders—from two different corps—was a costly miscue.)

Had everything gone right for the Confederates (an unlikely proposition), the best result that might have been achieved would have been the overrunning of Buford's final defensive position on McPherson's Ridge with light casualties prior to the arrival of Wadsworth's division of the I Corps. This would have forced the Federals to begin the fight on Cemetery Hill, perhaps as early as 11:00 A.M. Given the faster initial concentration of the Rebel army, there would have been a very good chance that by the time Meade had concentrated his army for battle he would have found Lee in possession of the entire "fish hook" down through the Round Tops. In such a circumstance it is not implausible to suggest that the new Federal army commander would have ordered a retreat to his Pipe Creek position. Tactically, that would have been a sound enough decision; politically, it is necessary to wonder whether Meade would have survived his first week of command.

That the Confederates required not just the morning but most of the afternoon to push the Federals off McPherson's Ridge was not, however, purely a function of their own mistakes. Three successive senior Union commanders— Buford, Reynolds, and Doubleday—made the same courageous decision to risk the survival of their entire command against the need to buy time for the army's concentration. Buford's defense in depth not only represented a textbook application of the concept, but also delayed the Confederate advance long enough for the first blue-clad infantry to arrive. Reynolds's dispositions in the crisis could be criticized on several counts (especially his placement of artillery and the piecemeal commitment of Cutler's brigade), but hard fighting by determined troops purchased another several hours on McPherson's Ridge. Doubleday's dispositions—for which he had the luxury of more time than Reynolds had been granted—were questionable in many respects, but tactical considerations were secondary to the fact that the acting corps commander decided to hazard any prolonged defense at all. Moreover, it is important to realize that given the numerical disparity under which he was forced to operate, it was unlikely that *any* defensive line that Doubleday could have created during the noon lull could have been held. Taken in sum, the senior Federal commanders performed significantly better than their Confederate counterparts; at least they sacrificed their men to a legitimate tactical end.

On the lower command levels the verdict was decidedly mixed. Poor performances by Cutler and Meredith were offset by the fumbling of Davis and Iverson. Outstanding tactical leadership by Baxter and Stone was equaled by Pettigrew and challenged by Daniel and Archer. As far as regimental commanders were concerned, dozens of officers on both sides distinguished themselves in the heavy fighting, often ending up among the casualties, though certainly Dawes of the 6th Wisconsin deserved special mention in that regard. As for the men themselves, Cutler's observation about his own regiments could well stand as the final commentary of their efforts; on both sides of the firing line the soldiers fought "as only brave men could fight. . . ."

Perhaps the most fascinating aspect of the day-long fight for McPherson's Ridge is the extent to which the peculiarities of the field dominated the flow of the battle. Willoughby Run and McPherson's Woods created an obstacle west of McPherson's Ridge that gave a decided advantage to the defenders, an advantage exploited not once but twice by the Federals. The railroad cut figured into the fate of several brigades on either side, serving almost as a magnet that drew the fighting down its banks. When the entire day is considered, however, it can be persuasively argued that the struggle for possession of that ditch prolonged the Federal defense of McPherson's Ridge; had it not been present, either Davis or Daniel might have unhinged the I Corps line.

In retrospect then, the Federal stand on McPherson's Ridge constituted an essential, if not critical component in the ultimate Union victory at Gettysburg. The Yankees eventually lost the high ground, but not before they had denied the Rebels their best chance to win the battle.

Touring the Battlefield

For most visitors to Gettysburg, viewing the area in which the struggle for McPherson's Ridge took place represents a secondary trip, often omitted if the day is too hot, too rainy, or the children in the back of the car grow too impatient for other pursuits. A reasonably fast-paced tour of that part of the battlefield, however, can be accomplished in a rewarding hour, and offers several opportunities for those with the time or the inclination to examine certain aspects of the field in depth. The instructions below follow the outline of a "quick tour," with additional (primarily walking) possibilities suggested at a number of stops.

Leave Gettysburg on U.S. Rt. 116 West, the old Fairfield/Hagerstown Road, and for the moment pass by Reynolds Avenue and Herr's Ridge Road, turning right on Black Horse Tavern Road. The vidette line of the 8th New York Cavalry would have been placed on the high ground to your right, and Marsh Creek parallels the road on the left. At about 1.6 miles you will turn right onto Knoxlyn Road; the vidette line of the 8th Illinois Cavalry will now be on your left.

Where Knoxlyn Road ends in a "T" intersection with U.S. Rt. 30 (Chambersburg Pike), there will be a small marker commemorating the first shot of the battle. Turn right on U. S. Rt. 30, and then take a quick left on Belmont Road. The vidette line of the 3rd Indiana Cavalry will be along the ground to your left, until you pass Black's Graveyard (c. 1740), where the unit that held the vidette line changed to

the 9th New York Cavalry. (While Devin's vidette line continued to the north and east, curling around Oak Hill, this
route will take you across the entire area through which
Heth's Division advanced on the morning of July 1.)

Turn right on Mummasburg Road, drive back toward
Gettysburg, and then turn right on Herr Ridge Road, which
you will follow across U.S. Route 30 back to U. S. 116. This
will take you along Herr Ridge, and Buford's planned skirmish line will be on your right. At the intersection of
Mummasburg Road and U.S. Route 30 Herr's Tavern will
be on your left. If you have been keeping odometer read-
ings, you will have noticed that the vidette line you traced
between the Hagerstown and Mummasburg Roads was
just over three miles long, but that the convergence of the
two roads has reduced the Herr Ridge line by nearly a mile.

Upon reaching U.S. Route 116 again you have traced
Buford's vidette and skirmish lines west of Gettysburg.
Turn left on U.S. Rt. 116, cross over Willoughby Run, and
turn left on Reynolds Avenue. You are now beginning to
examine McPherson's Ridge itself. Reynolds Avenue
between U.S. Rt. 116 and U.S. Rt. 30 is somewhat less than
one mile long, and this is an excellent part of the tour to
walk rather than drive (especially if you have someone
willing to take the car ahead for you). This will divorce
your tour of the field somewhat from the monument-by-
monument, start-and-stop driving that too often prevents
visitors from actually *seeing* the terrain.

As you walk, stop about every fifty yards for a deliberate
look both west and east. Peering west, down into the
woods along Willoughby Run, you will be struck by the
gentle incline of the western slope of McPherson's Ridge.
From the top of the ridge, it is difficult to imagine that
Buford—or anyone else—ever considered it a significant
piece of defensive terrain. When you look east, you will be
able to see the Seminary and northern Gettysburg quite
clearly, but what is again most striking is what you will *not*
see. Seminary Ridge, which looks so impressive on those

Present-day photo looking east from McPherson's Ridge at the Seminary. Seminary Ridge appears as just a slight undulation in the ground.

old "fuzzy caterpillar" maps, doesn't appear to be much more than an undulation in the ground. A little later you will discover that this apparent inconsequence is, in fact, an optical illusion, and that the ridgelines do convey significant advantages to their defenders. But what you will want to consider is the vast tactical experience and keen eye that allowed Buford, Gamble, and their men to realize almost immediately that this was critical ground.

As you note the monuments along Reynolds Avenue, be sure to stop at some of the cannon marking the location of various batteries. Stand behind them and take a gunner's view of Herr Ridge, trying to imagine just how distant the men of Archer's Brigade must have seemed on July 1, 1863. Then, still facing west, back up slowly until you are below the military crest of McPherson's Ridge. Note how quickly your view of Herr Ridge disappears, and think about the potential for passing an entire brigade east of McPherson's

Ridge without the Confederates ever seeing it. You will begin to understand why the appearance of the Iron Brigade created such consternation for the Rebels. Roughly two-thirds of the way down Reynolds Avenue toward U.S. Route 30, you will see McPherson's Woods on your left. The modern woods reach the road; in 1863 the trees probably did not come that far up the ridge. Walk down into the trees, realizing that—depending on the season of your particular tour—the foliage may have been thicker or thinner than you see it. In July 1863 there would have been a good canopy of leaves, and the trees would have been more densely packed than they appear today. This is an important observation, because, as you walk down the ridge toward the creek and then stop to look back, you may wonder how anyone could have missed a regiment or a brigade moving through those woods, especially when you can still see minivans coasting from statue to statue on Reynolds Avenue. Only part of the answer revolves around the changes that have taken place in the forest during the last century; you should also consider the effects of billowing clouds of black powder smoke from the initial skirmishing at Willoughby Run.

Stopping about fifty yards into the woods, turn right (north) and walk until you reach the rail fence that separates the trees from McPherson's Farm. The barn will be clearly visible just south of U.S. Rt. 30, and if you walk all the way down to the main road you will be able to get a close-up view of John Buford's monument. Be advised, however, that walking there and back again will cause you to hike about four hundred yards. Even if you do not make that longer trek, you will want to walk out into the field and look back toward McPherson's Ridge. All of a sudden, that inconsequential undulation (when viewed from its crest) begins to look a bit more formidable, and the cannon you can see (marking the position of Calef's guns) appear rather ominous. Head directly up the ridge, and if you are in shape (and not afraid to make something of a spectacle

Present-day photo of the typical fence seperating McPherson's Woods from the McPherson's farm.

of yourself for the tourists busily snapping photos of the monuments), try to maintain a double-quick time all the way up to the road. Be careful! This is a real field, complete with rocks and chuck holes. You will find yourself doing as much looking down as looking up, and you will quickly realize that the time it takes anyone (much less a regiment trying to maintain a line) to move from Willoughby Run to the top of McPherson's Ridge is quite significant. Veteran infantry would be able to get off quite a few volleys as your unit struggled up the ridge, to say nothing of cavalrymen with repeaters.

Back on Reynolds Avenue (either in your car or still walking), cross over U.S. Rt. 30 and stop at the modern bridge over the railroad cut. The railroad cut is probably the most interesting physical feature of the battlefield for younger children. Walk down the eastern slope of McPherson's Ridge about twenty yards, and very carefully approach the

Present-day photo of the railroad cut viewed from the east side of McPherson's Ridge. The bridge over the railroad is a modern-day addition.

edge of the cut. It is deep here, and the banks are far too steep to consider scaling (nor would the Gettysburg Battlefield Park want everyone clambering down and slowly destroying it), but you can safely get an excellent view of the cut as it slices through the ridge. You will realize that here, at least, the railroad cut hardly represented a good piece of defensive terrain; just maintaining your balance near the top of its banks would have been difficult enough, not to mention firing and reloading.

Now walk back up to Reynolds Avenue, cross the road carefully and examine the cut on the west side of the ridge. You will immediately notice that the height of the banks varies considerably as the ditch heads west. In several places the cut appears to be little deeper than the height of the average soldier. In all likelihood the precise variances have changed over the decades, but you will understand why—even along the front of a single regiment—some companies might have considered the railroad cut almost as good as a prepared entrenchment, while others considered it a death trap. This observation goes a long way toward explaining the success of Dawes's assault on Davis's Brigade.

Now return to Reynolds Avenue and continue moving north. After you have walked or driven about one hundred yards from the bridge over the railroad cut, stop and look at it from a distance. Voila! The entire railroad cut virtually disappears (especially if you manage to visualize the scene absent the new overpass). What you see is a line of trees and bushes winding in shallow curves up the slope. If you did not know that the railroad cut was there, you would probably assume that the foliage marked nothing more significant than a fence separating two fields. This observation will help you understand why, several times during the fighting, both Union and Confederate regiments marching on a north-south axis literally stumbled unawares into the railroad cut.

Continuing north on Reynolds Avenue, turn left onto Buford Avenue, and take that road north across Mummasburg Road to the Eternal Light Peace Memorial on Oak Hill. You will pass the monuments for a number of Buford's regiments, which can be confusing unless you realize that they were placed there not because of the fighting, but because they mark the location of the regimental camps on the night of June 30. At Oak Hill look north and you will see the woods in which Rodes's Division formed for its attack. To your right is where O'Neal's Alabama Brigade passed down the eastern slope of the ridge, completely out of Iverson's sight. When you leave Oak Hill, take Doubleday Avenue back toward Reynolds Avenue; notice the stone wall on your left. This is the wall from which Baxter's brigade rose up and commenced firing the volleys that mowed down Iverson's Tarheels. If you stop at the monument of the 12th Massachusetts, you will find a

Two of the monuments on McPherson's Ridge.

trail leading down to the point that the Federals seized three North Carolina battle flags. As you did west of McPherson's Ridge, walk down the slope a bit and get a feel for the terrain. You will notice the slight rolling of the ground that created small depressions in which a prone Confederate soldier might find some safety from devastating Union fire, but would be hopelessly pinned down—unable to attack or escape without exposing himself.

Follow Doubleday Avenue back to Reynolds Avenue, and when you reach the junction with U.S. Rt. 30 you will have finished your tour of the McPherson's Ridge section of the battlefield. If you take the entire tour by vehicle, with occasional stops at key points, the whole enterprise will consume about forty-five minutes. Should you possess the time, the interest, and the stamina for the walks suggested above, allow about two-and-one-half hours.

A final note: there are two reasons to tour a battlefield like McPherson's Ridge—commemoration and understanding. It is important to visit the monuments, read the names, and reflect on the ways that the men who fought at Gettysburg remembered the battle and their fallen comrades. Many of the monuments are striking works of art, and worthy of being included in your scrapbook. If, however, all or part of your intent is to understand the battle as the soldiers experienced it, you must look *away* from the memorials and concentrate on the terrain. Standing at their statues, align yourself to take in the same views that Buford, Reynolds, and Doubleday did, trying to visualize what they saw and felt on that hot July day, so many years ago.

Index

1st Brigade (Union 1st Cav. Div.; XI Corps) (Gamble), 17, 19
1st Brigade (Union 2nd Div.; I Corps) (Paul), 70, 83, 84
1st Brigade (Union 3rd Div.; I Corps) (C. Biddle), 70, 74, 97–98, 100
1st Cavalry Division (Buford), 13
1st Division (Union I Corps) (Wadsworth), 34–38, 69
1st New York Artillery, 74
1st Pennsylvania Artillery, 74
1st Tennessee, 26, 30, 31, 42
2nd Brigade (Union 1st Cav. Div.; XI Corps) (Devin), 17, 46, 79
2nd Brigade (Union 1st Div., I Corps) (Cutler), 36, 39, 40–41, 44, 48, 51–54, 55, 69–70, 87, 90
2nd Brigade (Union 2nd Div.; I Corps) (Baxter), 70, 72, 83
2nd Division (Union I Corps) (Robinson), 70, 83
2nd Maine Light Artillery (Hall), 31, 39, 41, 47–49, 51, 55
2nd Mississippi, 30, 45, 46–47, 51, 53, 54, 57, 59, 61
2nd North Carolina Battalion, 86, 89, 91
2nd U.S. Artillery (Calef), 19, 20
2nd Wisconsin, 36, 41, 42, 55, 69, 100
3rd Alabama, 81
III Corps (Conf.), 23, 24

3rd Division (Union I Corps) (Doubleday), 34, 35, 70
3rd Indiana, 17, 19, 105
3rd West Virginia, 17
4th U.S. Artillery, 74
5th Alabama, 23, 26, 30, 31, 81
5th Maine Battery, 74
5th North Carolina, 84
6th Alabama, 81
6th New York, 17
6th Wisconsin, 33–34, 36, 42, 56, 58, 59, 69, 100
7th Indiana, 36
7th Tennessee, 26, 30, 31, 42, 43, 55
7th Wisconsin, 36, 41, 42, 69, 98, 100
8th Illinois, 17, 19, 27, 105
8th New York, 17, 19, 105
9th New York, 17, 106
11th Mississippi, 30, 45
11th North Carolina, 76, 97, 100
11th Pennsylvania, 70, 83
12th Alabama, 81
12th Illinois, 17, 19
12th Massachusetts, 70, 83
12th North Carolina, 84, 89
13th Alabama, 23, 26, 27, 30, 31, 42
13th Massachusetts, 70
14th Brooklyn, 36, 41, 55, 56, 58, 69
14th Tennessee, 26, 30, 31, 42
16th Maine, 70
17th Pennsylvania, 17
19th Indiana, 36, 41, 42, 69, 97, 98

20th North Carolina, 78, 84
22nd Virginia Battalion, 76
23rd North Carolina, 84
24th Michigan, 36, 41–42, 69, 97, 98, 100
26th Alabama, 81
26th North Carolina, 76, 97, 98, 100
32nd North Carolina, 86, 93
40th Virginia, 76
42nd Mississippi, 30, 45, 46, 47–48, 49, 51, 55, 61
43rd North Carolina, 86
45th North Carolina, 86, 89, 91, 92
47th North Carolina, 76, 97, 100
47th Virginia, 43, 76, 100
52nd North Carolina, 76, 97, 100
53rd North Carolina, 86
55th North Carolina, 30, 45, 46, 51, 52, 53, 57, 61
55th Virginia, 76
56th Pennsylvania, 36, 41, 48, 51, 56, 69
76th New York, 36, 41, 51, 56, 69
80th New York, 70, 97
83rd New York, 70, 83
84th New York. *See* 14th Brooklyn
88th Pennsylvania, 70, 83
90th Pennsylvania, 70, 83
94th New York, 70
95th New York, 36, 41, 55, 56, 57, 58, 62, 69
97th New York, 70, 83
104th New York, 70
107th Pennsylvania, 70
121st Pennsylvania, 70, 97, 98
142nd Pennsylvania, 70
143rd Pennsylvania, 70, 87, 89, 92
147th New York, 36, 41, 48–49, 51, 52–54, 55, 69
149th Pennsylvania, 70, 87, 89, 92
150th Pennsylvania, 70, 74, 87, 95
151st Pennsylvania, 70, 97

Andrews, Hezekiah S., 91
Archer, James J., 23, 26–27, 29, 30, 31, 42–43, 104
Archer's Brigade, 23, 26–27, 28, 31, 41, 42–43, 55, 76

Battle, Cullen A., 81, 82
Baxter, Henry, 70, 82–85, 104
Beecham, Robert K., 42
Belo, Alfred H., 53, 57–59
Beveridge, John, 19
Biddle, Alexander, 97
Biddle, George H., 56
Biddle, Chapman, 70, 97–98
Bird, W. H., 42, 43
Blair, Major, 53, 57–59, 61
Boland, E. T., 27
Boyd, Samuel H., 91
Brabble, Edmund C., 93
Brockenbrough, John, 26, 30, 76, 95, 100
Buford, John, 13, 14–17, 18–20, 21, 22, 39, 69, 103
Burgwyn, Henry King, 100
Bynum, George, 45, 61
Bynum, Nathaniel, 45, 61
Bynum, Turner, 45, 61

Calef, John H., 19, 30–31
Cemetery Hill, 69
Chambersburg Pike, 27, 28, 30, 39, 46, 55, 70, 87, 89, 105
Chapman, George, 19
Christie, Daniel H., 84
Connally, John K., 46, 51, 53
Crawford, Will, 27
Crenshaw Artillery, 30
Cutler, Lysander, 35–36, 39, 40–41, 52–54, 69–70, 104

Dana, Amasa, 27
Dana, Edmund, 87
Daniel, Junius, 76, 81, 82, 89–93, 104

Daniel's Brigade, 81, 86, 89–93
Davis, Joseph R., 25–26, 27, 29,
    45–46, 52, 58, 104
Davis's Brigade, 28, 30, 45–52, 56,
    57, 58–61, 75, 101
Dawes, Rufus R., 33–34, 42, 56–57,
    59, 61, 104
Devin, Thomas C., 17, 20, 46
Doles, George, 79
Doles's Brigade, 79, 81
Dorsett, James, 100
Doubleday, Abner, 21, 34–35, 43,
    56, 65–70, 72–74, 95, 101,
    103–104
Dudley, William, 98
Dwight, Walton, 87, 93

Ellsworth, Timothy, 53

Fairchild, Lucius, 41, 42
Fowler, Edward, 41, 55, 56
Fredericksburg Artillery, 30
Fry, Birkett D., 27, 76
Fulton, William F., 23

Gamble, William, 17–18, 28–29
Gambrell, J. B., 46–47
Gates, Theodore, 97
George, Newton, 26
Grover, Andrew, 51–52

Hall, James A., 31, 39–40, 41, 48,
    49, 51
Hankins, Samuel, 46, 47, 51, 57
Harney, George, 52–53
Harris, Lloyd G., 57
Herbst Woods. *See* McPherson's
    Woods
Herr Ridge, 17, 19, 20, 28, 29, 41,
    47, 74, 75, 76, 89, 106, 107
Heth, Henry, 24–25, 27, 29–30, 43,
    75–76, 95, 97, 102
Heth's Division, 23–24, 100–101
Hill, A. P., 74–75

Hood, T. C., 100
Hopkins, J.A., 92

Iron Brigade, 31, 33, 36–38, 41–42,
    54, 55, 57, 58, 69–70, 95, 98–100
Iverson, Alfred, 76, 77–79, 81, 82,
    83, 84, 85, 89, 104
Iverson's Brigade, 81, 83, 84,
    89–90

Jerome, Aaron, 17
Johnston, Andrew, 30
Jones, Marcellus, 21–22

Kelly, James, 59
Kress, John, 22, 41–42

Lee, Robert E., 75
Leventhorpe, Collett, 100

Mahoney, Patrick, 43
Mansfield, John, 42, 43
Markell, William, 19
Marye, Edward, 30
Mayo, Robert M., 100
McPherson's Ridge, 9, 17, 19, 29,
    40, 41,42, 47, 51, 67, 68–73,
    102–103, 105, 106–113
McPherson's Woods, 19, 30, 31,
    55, 68, 69, 70, 95, 98–99, 104, 108
Meade, George G., 12, 13, 21, 38,
    65, 66
Meredith, Solomon, 34, 36–37, 41,
    56, 69, 95, 98, 104
Miller, Francis, 41, 48
Miller, Hugh R., 46, 47–48, 51, 52
Morrow, Henry, 42, 98
Murphy, William B., 59
Musser, John D., 92

Newton, John M., 65

Oak Hill, 79, 81, 89, 111
Oak Ridge, 79, 81, 82, 83

O'Neal, Edward A., 81, 82, 84

Paul, Gabriel, 70, 83, 84, 85
Pease, Francis, 51
Pegram, William J., 30, 74
Pender, William Dorsey, 24
Pettigrew, Johnston J., 25, 30, 76,
    100, 102, 104
Pierce, J. Volney, 51, 53
Pye, Edward, 56, 57

Railroad cut, 46, 56–63, 91–93,
    104, 109–111
Reynolds Avenue, 11, 106–109,
    110, 111
Reynolds, John F., 13–14, 15, 21,
    34–35, 38–39, 43–44, 68, 103
Robinson, John C., 34, 70
Robinson, William, 42, 98
Rodes, Robert, 75, 79, 81, 102
Rodes's Division, 79–86, 111
Rowley, Thomas, 70

Seminary Ridge, 18, 40, 49, 52, 67,
    68–69, 70, 79, 107
Slagle, Jacob, 68

Stevens, George, 42
Stone, Colonel, 46, 51
Stone, Roy, 70, 87–89, 90, 104
Stone's Brigade, 70, 76, 87–93

Tunney, J. B., 27

Vairin, Augustus, 47, 57
Van de Graaf, Arthur, 23–24, 27

Wadsworth, James, 21, 34–35, 39,
    40, 41, 49, 73, 87
Wainwright, Charles S., 74, 97
Wallar, Francis A., 59
Williams, Oliver, 84
Williams, Samuel, 42
Willoughby Run, 12, 19, 29, 30, 31,
    55, 69, 87, 95, 104, 106, 108
Wills, David, 62
Wister, Langhorne, 87, 92–93
Worley, C. L. F., 28
Wright, Nathaniel, 53
Wyburn, William, 53

Young, Albert, 56